Divers Tongues

by Ron Crawford

Pneumatikos Publishing
P.O. 595351
Dallas, TX 75359

Info@pneumatikos.com

© 2001 by Ron Crawford

Published by Pneumatikos Publishing
P.O. Box 595351
Dallas, TX 75359
E-mail: info@pneumatikos.com
www.pneumatikos.com

First printing, November 2001

Printed in the United States of America. All rights reserved under International Copyright Law. No part of this publication may be reproduced, stored in a retrieval system or transmitted in any form or by any means--for example, electronic, photocopy, recording--without the prior written permission of the publisher. The only exception is brief quotations for printed reviews.

ISBN #0-9712249-4-3

Excel Digital Press
P.O. Box 703978
Dallas, TX 75370

Cover Art Work by Fabian Arroyo

Unless otherwise noted, Scripture quotations are from the HOLY BIBLE, Authorized King James Version.

Table of Contents

Introduction	1
1 — Divers Tongues	7
2 — A Spiritual Office	17
3 — The Divers Classification	25
4 — The Modern Day Church	33
5 — A Need For Present Truth	43
6 — A Current Conversion	51
7 — Most Holy Faith	63
8 — Divers Intercession	69
9 — A Different Kind Of Prayer Meeting	75
10 — A Different Kind Of Intercessor	89
11 — Of Men And Of Angels	103
12 — A Different Kind Of Warfare	113
13 — A Different Kind Of Worship	131
14 — A More Excellent Way	141

Acknowledgements

Thanks to all who have patterned the lessons learned concerning divers tongues. Your intercession and faithfulness to the Lord has been and still is a constant source of encouragement and strength.

I want to thank my wife, Debbie, and my daughters Kelly and Katy for allowing me to go to bed early and arise before dawn in order to write many of these chapters. Your love and understanding, along with your prayers and belief, have sustained and inspired my efforts. Always remember how much I love you.

To the remnant of my church who have withstood pressures and attacks and still abide faithful to the Lord and His call, thank you for your devotion to the Lord and your willingness to follow us as we follow Christ.

I want to thank the proofreaders David Wright, Tammy Stewart, Sondra Carter, Monica Terrill, and especially Shawn Magill.

I want to thank Joy Harrison, our business administrator, whose determination and commitment to the development of this book and the other works of Pneumatikos Publishing has been invaluable.

To Stacy Masten, chief editor, may God mightily reward you for the untold hours and energies that you freely devoted to Him in this ministry of writing.

I want to thank Paul Harrison, my brother in Christ, colleague and fellow witness of the pathways of the Lord, for being a faithful servant of the Lord Jesus. Your life and walk have truly been a constant inspiration to me. Now I know why the Lord sent them forth "two by two." Agreement, yes; but it also helps to know that there is at least one other person that is just foolish enough to believe the Lord no matter what.

And most importantly, I want to thank My Heavenly Father. You are my source of life and love, and I am so grateful that you allow me to know you. Thank you for giving me the privilege of praying and seeking your heart and for revealing tools of commune that afford me the privilege of seeking you with increasingly greater passion. Thank you for allowing me to share some of these tools in this book.

Thank you all.
Pastor Ron Crawford

Preface

There are many in the Christian world that would attest to the Biblical topic of the baptism in the Holy Spirit; however, there are some who are strongly and adamantly opposed to this Scriptural teaching. When it comes down to it, the Bible speaks about many things that Christians have no working knowledge or, at best, a minimal understanding. One topic is the Biblical validity of divers tongues. This is a crucial mystery that God has revealed in this hour. The Son of God spoke about such revelations:

> *At that time Jesus answered and said, I thank thee, O Father, Lord of heaven and earth, because thou hast* **hid** *[apokalupto] these things from the wise and prudent, and hast revealed them unto babes. Even so, Father: for so it seemed good in thy sight."* Matthew 11:25-26

The Greek word *apokalupto* means a mystery that has been covered or hidden. Only babes, or those with child-like wonder and faith, will see them. The mysteries will remain hidden to those who deem themselves wise and prudent concerning the things of God.

I used to be this way. When I was initially baptized in the Holy Spirit, I spoke in unknown tongues. I was convinced that this was all there was; therefore, God's ability to reveal anything new to me was hindered. Then, my wife and I began visiting Pastor Crawford's church. During the worship services, there was a depth of spiritual language that was foreign to me, and it made me hungry for more of God and for the gift that He was revealing in that house. That gift was divers tongues.

Understanding and utilizing this gift has revolutionized my Christian walk. There is a greater depth to my commune with the Heavenly Father, and my spiritual understanding has increased. Doors of revelation have opened up in ways that I never thought possible. I began to consistently have dreams and visions and encounters with His mighty angels. Divers tongues activated my heart to believe God for anything.

Ron Crawford brings to light the experiential reality of the gift of divers tongues. This is a vital truth that God has wonderfully revealed to this man of God in these last days. This pastor is a devoted intercessor and daily exemplifies a life of holiness before his family and church. His church is filled with people who demonstrate the reality of divers tongues.

As you read this book, listen for the heartbeat of the Father resounding within your spirit. **Divers Tongues** should create a hunger in your heart for more of the Lord. Open your heart and let God explode this powerful truth into your spirit. I believe this is one of many insights that God is releasing into His church in these last days.

Evangelist Mark E. Burke
Lakewood Assembly of God, Dallas, Texas

INTRODUCTION

TAKE EVERYTHING THAT YOU KNOW ABOUT YOUR RELATIONSHIP WITH GOD AND SET IT ASIDE FOR JUST A MOMENT. LOOK AT IT INTENTLY AND KNOW THAT GOD WANTS TO CHANGE MOST OF IT – RIGHT NOW.

The above statement will either inspire you or offend you. Your reaction will determine whether God will be able to move within you in the way in which He has desired. Whether you are a believer in Christ Jesus or a person who has never truly known Him, God wants to radically draw you closer to Him. His heart longs for you, and He wants you to be found in Him.

Two Essentials

In order to please God, you must begin with two things: a willingness to do whatever He asks and an obedience that is ready to respond affirmatively to Him. The absence of either of these will corrupt and endanger your relationship with Him. Relationship with God is what we were created to enjoy. Since the fall of Adam, God has committed Himself to the purposes of restoring commune with mankind.

The Scenario

Just about everybody thinks that they know all that they need to know about God. Christians excel at telling non-Christians that there is a God who wants to know them. Who tells this message to the Christian? Who is the exhorter to the pew?

Communion with God is to be our function, not our option. Fellowshipping with Him is a necessity, not a discretionary pursuit. God is longing for those who will seek to know Him intimately. He is drawing individuals to His Throne in order to develop them into partners. There are exploits that must be accomplished on this planet and in the heavens, and He will only share them with those who remain close to Him.

Divers tongues is the compelling capacity to communicate with God in any and every dimension. It is the capability wherewith God empowers His church to apostolically proceed in new and mighty realms of commune.

> *For our conversation is in heaven; from whence also we look for the Saviour, the Lord Jesus Christ:*
> *Philippians 3:20*

Language Of The Heavenlies

We live in a communication age. We avidly acquire state-of-the-art technology that will allow us to link and remain current with society, business, and every other form of interface. Since the day Thomas Edison spoke his now-

Introduction

famous words to Watson and the telephone was born, people have longed to communicate in unfettered fashion.

Advances in communication have always preceded and defined progress in the history of man. Smoke signals were made obsolete by the telegraph wire. The wire soon morphed from Morse code to vocal; wire became wireless; land-based became airwave; and airwave yielded to digital satellite. Why did all of this happen? Mankind continually seeks to communicate in an increasingly clear and more effective manner. In fact, a passion within man insists on the latest and best.

God offers to us a magnificent opportunity that transcends anything we have known in the natural. It also revolutionizes the communication capacities that we have previously known in the spirit realm. It is new, yet very old. Divers tongues is God's communications strategy for this day. He offers it to us on the basis of His Word and purpose.

Where Has Divers Tongues Been All These Centuries?

When the New Testament spoke of divers tongues, the Church was a progressive and pioneering entity. When the Church became dormant and monastic in its existence, divers tongues disappeared.

Divers was not alone in this tragic development as most of the power giftings of the Spirit were lost due to complacency and lack of vision within the Church. This occurred because dormancy of man and the propensity to exist on yesterday's victory. The enemy encouraged this death sentence, and the gifts of the Spirit were relegated to the lore of yesterday's dispensation.

At the turn of the twentieth century, unknown tongues was rediscovered by many within the Church. Places like Topeka, Kansas, and Azusa Street became watchwords of a fresh visitation of God wherein speaking in other tongues was sought after and thousands were baptized with the Holy Spirit. Throughout the decades of the 1900s, God progressively revealed Himself through visitations. We are currently in the apostolic age, and the communication capacity for this time is now being made available to those who are hungry for more of God. Divers tongues is here!

Within this book, you will be presented with many aspects of communing with God that can only be accessed by virtue of a passion for Him and His ways. Divers tongues will cause you to be able to flow in dynamic fashion within the heart of God. This will empower you to minister in diverse realms and dimensions of His choosing.

You need to be filled with the capacity for divers tongues. If you are a "spirit filled" believer, you need to ask God to impart divers tongues to you. If you have not been filled with the Spirit with the evidence of speaking with other tongues, you need to ask Jesus to baptize you in the Holy Ghost and begin to speak according to the pattern of Scripture.

Introduction

> *He said unto them, Have ye received the Holy Ghost since ye believed? And they said unto him, We have not so much as heard whether there be any Holy Ghost.*
>
> *And when Paul had laid his hands upon them, the Holy Ghost came on them; and they spake with tongues, and prophesied.*
>
> *Acts 19:2, 6*

If you are not a born-again believer in Jesus Christ, you need to ask Him into your life right now. Ask the Heavenly Father to forgive your sins because of the death of Jesus on the cross of Calvary. Ask God to accept you into His family and welcome the new life of Christ that came through Jesus' cross and resurrection.

> *That if thou shalt confess with thy mouth the Lord Jesus, and shalt believe in thine heart that God hath raised him from the dead, thou shalt be saved.*
>
> *Romans 10:9*

Maybe you have been hungry for the things of the Spirit. Perhaps you have sought for meaning in your life and have not found the fullness that you long to know. There is no power in religion, and there is no meaning in New Age. The psychic realm will only introduce you to the fact that there is a supernatural realm.

God is calling to you through His Son. The supernatural gifting that is within you was given to you by Him, and he wants to access and develop those capacities of your spiritual life. Why settle for a weak imitation of the real thing?

God wants YOU. You really want and need Him, too.

This book is about a gift that will help you to fellowship with the Most High in a most remarkable fashion. God's ways are new every morning, and divers tongues will help you to enter into those ways and communicate within them. Divers tongues is God's gift for today!!!

chapter 1

Divers Tongues

Background Check

As a classic Pentecostal from my youth, I learned the dogma of Pentecost. Raised in the Assemblies of God, I heard the defining principles declared with regularity: "There is a subsequent experience to salvation, and it is known as the baptism of the Holy Ghost with the initial physical evidence of speaking with other tongues." Every full gospel believer is familiar with that statement and truth.

I was "born again" at age five. I was filled with the Spirit during junior high school. Once I received my "prayer language," that same tongue remained with me through Bible college, seminary, and sixteen years of pastoral ministry.

Then, it happened! My entire framework of understanding regarding Pentecost, and my experience therein, changed. God welcomed me into the realm of divers tongues. Hallelujah!

Funny thing about it is, I was not looking to change anything. Isn't that usually the case? Wanting more of God, seeking revival, and singing songs about being changed; yet, in reality, not expecting to change.

The Brownsville Revival

In 1996, the Lord launched my church into a dynamic retooling that followed a visit to Pensacola, Florida. God had been moving mightily for many months in an Assemblies of God church named Brownsville, and His move in that city had already generated international interest. Little did I know that the visit of my church staff to the site of this phenomenon would change my life and my church forever.

I had been serving as the Senior Pastor of a well-established Assemblies church for seven years. I was happy from the standpoint of outward appearance. God had blessed me with a lovely wife, two precious daughters and a prospering fellowship to shepherd. Our church was enjoying a season of marvelous blessing. We employed an excellent staff of ministers. Every department was growing to the degree that we were entertaining plans for the expansion of our church plant. From the outward appearance, we were a model church. On the inside, I knew that we were spiritual weaklings. A strange stirring had been in my heart for months, a stirring that led me to fasting and prayer. My expression to God was simple: "I must have more of you, Lord. This pleasant existence is what I have labored to attain, but I know there is more than this. It involves knowing you more and I will do whatever it takes to find it."

When my fast ended, God led me to call our congregation to fast and pray. Our aspiration was elemental on the surface. We simply asked God to help us to find Him. Our cry was to know Him in ways that we had never known Him. Sounds great, doesn't it? Don't ever ask God for these things unless you really mean it and are willing to pay the cost of your very life.

In November of 1996, God graciously arranged for my staff and me to attend a pastor's conference at Brownsville. The power of God was resident in that place, and we were all mightily touched. This would mark the beginning of an incredible journey.

My Introduction To Divers Tongues

On the first Sunday morning after we returned from the pastor's conference in November, I spoke about the glorious things that God had done. At the end of the service, one of the board members whom I had known for many years came to greet me. I wasn't prepared for his initial comment. It went something like this: "Pastor, your tongue has changed." He subsequently elaborated that he and his wife were amazed at this because they had become accustomed to hearing me speak in the same unknown tongue for years. On that morning, they told me I spoke in a different language. This report surprised me, to say the least.

After greeting a few more people, I made my way to the seclusion of my office. Sheltered safely within those walls, I began to pray in the Spirit. To my amazement, I not only spoke in a new tongue but also in many varying types of tongues. This happened during the course of a several-minute interchange with God. How could this be? What did this mean? I had to know!

Unknown Tongues

Any Pentecostal who is truly candid will admit that once you attain a "prayer language," it usually becomes as familiar to you as your own voice. You may not know what you are communicating to God, but the sounds are familiar.

Growing up in a Pentecostal church, I became aware of the classic nuances accompanying the "unknown" tongues of those within that church. Sister Brown spoke in that language. Brother Clark sounds this way. Billy's Mom has unusual characteristics of tongues that often embarrass him. These patterns never seemed to change.

Doctrinal Understandings

We came by our doctrinal position honestly and sincerely. We learned how to be filled and what it meant to be filled. We learned what it meant to pray in the Spirit.

We learned the rules of how to give a "message in tongues," and we often endured the same person giving the same kind of message in the same way with the same "Genesis to Revelation" interpretation. On the way home from church after such an eruption, Mom and Dad would speak of how such frustrated "lay preachers" needed their own pulpit. In the same light, they would check the box score to see if we had exceeded the "three-message rule" (1 Corinthians 14:27). In that discussion, we always kept in mind that a message and interpretation equaled prophecy (1 Corinthians 14:5).

Our world of the unknown rarely changed much. The unknown was not only known, but also predictable. The mysterious had now become a puzzle whose pieces were forever shellacked into place. That's <u>what doctrine does – it crystallizes experience in the light of Scripture.</u> The Scripture was never meant to be crystallized. The things of the Spirit of God should be timeless and current at the same time. When the deep things of God become common, it is a sign that we must probe deeper.

Babies And Bath Water

In no way am I ridiculing the atmosphere in which I was spiritually raised. It is nothing short of wondrous to realize how God has launched the message of Pentecost during the past century.

Yet God is not constrained by His examples of past revelation. As I searched the Scripture for the meaning of what was happening to me, the Lord directed me to many well-known passages. I began to see these passages in a new light. The Holy Spirit was now breathing new understanding into Scripture that I had studied and preached in the past. In many ways, it was as if I was converted and reading the Bible for the first time.

I have heard it said that when Christian churchgoers complain that the Word of God is not being preached, it often means that the underlined passages in *their* Bible are not being recounted. For me, I began to read those underlined passages with a fresh verve, as well as the others that had previously been unexplored. My explanation for what was happening to me was found in one of those underlined passages.

Definition Of The Gift

It is traditionally believed that the modern church was born on the day of Pentecost. At this time, God gave the Church the gift of speaking in other tongues as stated in Acts.

> *And they were all filled with the Holy Ghost, and began to speak with other tongues, as the Spirit gave them utterance.*
>
> *Acts 2:4*

Speaking in tongues became the norm for the early church. This is born out by an examination of Acts 19 when Paul asked the Ephesian church if they had received the Holy Ghost since they believed:

> *And it came to pass, that, while Apollos was at Corinth, Paul having passed through the upper coasts came to Ephesus: and finding certain disciples, [2] He said unto them, Have ye received the Holy Ghost since ye believed? And they said unto him, We have not so much as heard whether there be any Holy Ghost. [3] And he said unto them, Unto what then were ye baptized? And they said, Unto John's baptism. [4] Then said Paul, John verily baptized with the baptism of repentance, saying unto the people, that they should believe on him which should come after him, that is, on Christ Jesus.*

[5] When they heard this, they were baptized in the name of the Lord Jesus. [6] And when Paul had laid his hands upon them, the Holy Ghost came on them; <u>and they spake with tongues, and prophesied.</u>

Acts 19:1-6

Paul spoke to the Corinthian church of additional gifts given to an existing spirit-filled congregation.

For to one is given by the Spirit the word of wisdom; to another the word of knowledge by the same Spirit; [9] To another faith by the same Spirit; to another the gifts of healing by the same Spirit; [10] To another the working of miracles; to another prophecy; to another discerning of spirits; to another divers kinds of tongues; to another the interpretation of tongues.

I Corinthians 12:8-10

These additional **gifts** are identified as ***charismata*** in the original Greek language. Literally, ***charismata*** means "with grace," and describes the way that the Holy Spirit blesses the church with unexpected provision and victory. Grace is God's way of delivering us from calamity or desperate situations. Grace is also given by God when He desires to promote us into a higher mode of living and service to Him. His Throne is one that is comprised of grace, and His purposes are communicated by virtue of dispensations of grace.

These "grace" gifts are not normal in their scope. For instance, the grace gift of faith is not simply a hyped up belief. The grace gifts of healings are not simply an extension of the covenant blessing that we already enjoy. These "graces" are explosive visitations from the Spirit of the Lord. They are not "re-packagings" of what is already known. God delights in giving these creative types of provision and experience to His children.

When it comes to divers tongues, most Pentecostals would readily declare that this gift has already been given to them by virtue of their initial baptism in the Spirit. However, God is so creative that He does not need to re-package something that we already have and should be utilizing to the fullest.

Divers tongues is a gift of the Spirit that is mightier than we can possibly imagine. Its usage provides a remarkable and intimate dimension of commune with the Father. There are insights that can only come through reception and utilization of this powerful gift. Divers tongues is a different gifting than the general gift of tongues. It operates more fluently and generates a more powerful scope of influence.

Scope Of The Gift

God's Word never promised us "a prayer language," yet we have settled for that singular experience. For instance, I can hear someone speak in their prayer language and know if they were filled during the charismatic movement, the faith movement of the seventies or during various other emphases of the Holy Ghost. This is a terrific beginning, but that was years ago.

Divers tongues utilizes the foundation of speaking in tongues; however, there will be marked changes in dialogue and language. Divers tongues will not be predictable but will flow as the Spirit leads into different languages spontaneously. This will result in greater power for intercession. Revelatory giftings will also be birthed and activated, and angelic interaction will increase as a benefit of speaking in divers tongues. There will even be those who function in the office of divers tongues.

Divers tongues will revolutionize the life of the individual believer. A proper ascertaining of the Scripture will also empower the Church in ways that have been shrouded by ignorance.

Receiving Divers Tongues

When God began to visit our congregation with the blessing of divers tongues, we were absolutely surprised by the gift. We had no preconceived pursuit of such a blessing as we did not have any idea that such a thing could be known. So many of our people simply began speaking in varied languages in the Spirit and it was our privilege to utilize this gift in our intercession.

As others heard of the wonderful things God was doing, they desired to receive God's touch in a similar way. We simply laid hands on them and prayed, asking God to grant divers tongues in the same mode that he granted general tongues. The Scriptural pattern worked wonderfully for us as it will for you.

chapter 2

A Spiritual Office

A Gift Of The Spirit

When we explore the gifts of the Spirit in the writings of the Apostle Paul, we have often misinterpreted the intent of the Holy Ghost because of our lack of understanding regarding tongues and the gift of divers tongues.

As we look with an open heart at 1 Corinthians 12, we see a startling truth that both Pentecostals and non-Pentecostals miss. Paul begins to list offices or ministerial giftings of apostles, prophets and teachers that the Father has placed in the Church. In the same breath, Paul proceeds to declare that there is also a similar ministerial function for miracle working, gifts of healings, helps, governments and divers tongues.

> *Now ye are the body of Christ, and members in particular. [28] And God hath set some in the church, first apostles, secondarily prophets, thirdly teachers, after that miracles, then gifts of healings, helps, governments, diversities of tongues.*
> *1 Corinthians 12:27-28*

Within this crucial framework, Paul lists divers tongues as appropriate for consideration alongside such offices as prophets, teachers and apostles. One of the purposes of this book is to establish the validity of an office of divers tongues that has equal standing and import with that of the other offices listed.

Removing Restrictions

In the very next verse Paul asks, *"Are all apostles?"* (1 Corinthians 12:29). He was in no way disallowing the office of the apostle. He was simply shining a light on the fact that not everyone is an apostle, but they do exist. This is a sovereign assignment by the Father to certain people. Then he asks about prophets, teachers, workers of miracles and possessors of gifts of healings. He was declaring the existence of such empowerment within the ministries of certain individuals who are called by Him to work within these offices.

> *But all these worketh that one and the selfsame Spirit, dividing to every man severally as he will.*
> *1 Corinthians 12:11*

Do All Speak With Tongues?

When we view the above in the light of revelation, it removes a perplexing thought for many classic Pentecostals. This new light also removes a glaring excuse from the vocabulary of many anti or neutral "non" tongue-talkers. In 1 Corinthians 12:30 Paul asks if all speak with tongues and interpretation. This has been a shelter of inactivity and a clause for exemption from speaking in tongues. The argument against everyone speaking in tongues as a general gifting of the Holy Spirit will find a marginal legitimacy in the fuller understanding of this verse. We readily see that Paul was not talking about the gift of tongues, but the office and ministry of divers tongues. This opens a whole new realm of understanding.

The writer of this chapter is the very same Apostle who came to the Ephesians and insisted that the disciples within that community be filled with the Spirit with the evidence of speaking in tongues as shown in Acts 19. It is therefore hard to fathom that this same Apostle would soften his insistence that *every* believer speak with unknown tongues. While everyone is to be filled with the Holy Spirit and to speak in tongues, not everyone is called to the office of divers tongues. This understanding flows in the context of Paul's writings and removes a perceived contradiction of terms.

How The Office Works

A Scriptural office fulfills a function on an ongoing basis. It is not sporadic in demonstration. In our world, if we go to a business office, the specialization of that business is transacted. Whatever the shingle on the door advertises is what we can expect to find inside. For example, in the office of a bank, we can expect to find banking going on inside. The agents of the business have both rules of conduct in representing headquarters as well as latitude in transacting business.

It is this way with the offices of the Lord as He conducts His business within them. The office of divers tongues is no exception. It has a consistent purpose, responsibility, functionality, power and discretionary flow.

What The Office Offers

Whenever someone flows in this office, they have the capacity to demonstrate *all* of the function of that gift as the Lord directs. An illustration of this power and discretion can be found in the comparison of the prophetic gift versus the prophetic office. According to 1 Corinthians 14:31, *"ye may all prophesy one by one,"* and should; however, a "prophet" lives a lifestyle of prophecy. While the prophetic word can come powerfully through any believer, the prophetic office has a greater and more consistent anointing that abides within the person who fills that office. So it is with divers tongues.

As it was with the school of the prophets in Old Testament days, so it is with any office of God. There will be a definite focus on the office wherever it abides. For example, if a church has a prophetic office anointing, those who visit that church will become partakers of that resident anointing and should be changed by virtue of that exposure. There is an impartation that takes place. So it is with divers tongues.

"Is Saul also among the prophets?" should be the watchword of modern day offices of the Lord. Saul could prophesy but was not a prophet (1 Samuel 10:11-12). Offices and predominant callings are that way. So it is with divers tongues.

Unto Men

How then can the office of divers tongues benefit the Body of Christ? Can anyone operate therein? The answer is yes and no. Everyone can flow in divers tongues, but not everyone will stand in the office.

One of the glaring difficulties within the modern church is the desire to be *everything*. An old adage from the business world tells young entrepreneurs to "discover what you are good at and do it. Find a need, fill it well, and the world will beat a path to your door."

Most churches do not know what their primary gifting or function is within the Body of Christ. They are busily involved in the pursuit of being everything, and/or keeping up with the newest thrust of emphasis Body-wide.

However, this is the way it should work. Each believer should realize his or her gift and purpose and exercise it. This meets the individual need and the needs of the local Body. When a church knows what its primary function is within the Body of Christ, it should fulfill it effectively. Just as in the human body, adjoining parts should coordinate with each other and supply what is required for health and vitality. Paul emphasized this truth when he said:

> *If the whole body* were *an eye, where* were *the hearing? If the whole* were *hearing, where* were *the smelling?*
> *1 Corinthians 12:17*

Offices of cooperative influence will often be housed together. For instance, the divers office will also have a mighty influence of interpretation and prophecy within its domain. There should also be an operational representation of the other offices of the Father within that church.

At times, like cross-pollination, the Lord will touch His offices with anointings from people or churches that flow in other offices. This can happen through visitation of guest ministers or through joint attendance at conferences or conventions. Each office or joint supplies.

People who are assigned within a house where the divers office abides will exhibit a great propensity for praying and declaring in divers tongues. Those who visit with an open heart and mind, and especially those who come expectantly, will begin to flow in divers tongues. Subsequently, they will grow in the gift and spread the effect to their local place of ministry.

Every Spirit-baptized believer has the capacity to pray in tongues and in divers tongues. The location of the office is by the direction of the Father, but everyone who believes can enjoy the fruit of the office.

chapter 3

The Divers Classification

Genos

Of all the words that the Holy Ghost could have utilized to typify **divers**, He chose the word *genos*. We have generally interpreted **divers** as simply meaning multiple or varied in some way, but the word *genos* in the original Greek means so much more. Most generally, it is used to describe particular people groups or nations; however, more broadly, it implies the notion of differing lands or species as well. So why would God choose this word to define the gift of multiple tongues? Consider with me some New Testament citings of this word.

We Are Given A Lineage Through Our Heavenly Father

> *Forasmuch then as we are the* **offspring** [genos] *of God, we ought not to think that the Godhead is like unto gold, or silver, or stone, graven by art and man's device.*
>
> *Acts 17:29*

We are the *genos* of God! God characterizes us as His offspring and generation. An offspring can only come through a birthing. Birthing consists of many steps in the natural, and none of them are optional. It is the same way in the spirit realm. Passion, conception, gestation, travail, birthing, establishing of new life – these are all initiated and generated through intercession and declaration in divers tongues.

The implication and reality of this is much, much deeper. God desires for us to be a people who are His heirs and who have dominion and represent Him on this planet. Divers tongues provides us with the opportunity to speak in God's language to whatever part of that dominion He wants to activate or to be utilized. Ultimately, this will encompass His purposes through our Lord Jesus Christ.

The Kingly Line Of David Through The Lineage Of Christ

> *I Jesus have sent mine angel to testify unto you these things in the churches. I am the root and the* **offspring** *[genos] of David, and the bright and morning star.*
> *Revelation 22:16*

> *But ye are a chosen* **generation** *[genos], a royal priesthood, an holy nation, a peculiar people; that ye should shew forth the praises of him who hath called you out of darkness into his marvellous light.*
> *1 Peter 2:9*

We are the offspring of God only through the wondrous gift of our Lord Jesus Christ. When we are born into the family of God, it is only because of and through the Lord Jesus Christ. As His bloodline, we define the heritage of King David.

Genos involves heritage. In this passage, a link between *genos* and the lineage of David in Christ is declared. The redeemed family of God believes for the re-establishment of the Tabernacle of David according to Amos 9:11. This is a place of unhindered and expressive praise to the Most High God. Divers tongues will be a prominent feature of the ongoing operation of this tabernacle. The ministry of the angels of the Lord will also be paramount in every facet of this establishment. Jesus declared that His angels would testify of these things.

As ministers within this glorious tabernacle, we are called to be a royal priesthood. New sounds of heaven will be heard on this planet, and God will be exalted above the clouds. Our Heavenly Father intends for this earth to be filled with the knowledge and glory of the Lord.

Thus implemented, a holy or saintly nation of believers will be formed. This incredible and dynamic type of believer in Jesus Christ is already being prepared for the coming days. These individuals will be peculiar and unlike anything else that the world has to offer.

Divers Tongues In The Church

As we previously discussed, individual giftings are made available to the believer on a personal basis through a grace gift of the Holy Ghost:

> *To another the working of miracles; to another prophecy; to another discerning of spirits; to another* divers **kinds** [genos] *of tongues; to another the interpretation of tongues.*
> *1 Corinthians 12:10*

These "best gifts" will be granted for use as the Spirit deems necessary. Perhaps the intercessory need of the moment requires the issuance of divers capacity, or maybe the needed declaration in the spirit realm surpasses the regular quotient of communication.

God often visits individuals with a grace gift to see if they are willing to move within that capacity on a regular basis. How they react and utilize the opportunity in the Lord will determine whether the Lord can use them in similar fashion in the future. Grace is a continual pathway of growth and development in the Lord.

The corporate gifting of divers tongues is made available through the offices that are set within the framework of the structure of the church:

> *And God hath set some in the church, first apostles, secondarily prophets, thirdly teachers, after that miracles, then gifts of healings, helps, governments,* **diversities** *[genos] of tongues.*
> *1 Corinthians 12:28*

These gifts are given by the Lord Jesus as pointed out in Ephesians 4:11. Our Lord includes divers tongues as an office of the church. These offices are located in strategic places on the earth.

The Kingdom Of Heaven Works Through A Divers Process

Whenever the phrase the "Kingdom of Heaven" comes to your mind, what does it make you think of? If those thoughts do not involve what God is transacting right now and how you can partner with Him in that plan, you need to study the topic in Scripture. Consider one verse, for example:

> *And from the days of John the Baptist until now the kingdom of heaven suffereth violence, and the violent take it by force.*
> *Matthew 11:12*

Have you been violent for the Kingdom lately? This verse says that God's Kingdom has been violently appropriated by the enemy, who wrongfully forced his way into positions where he did not belong. God is looking for a people who will move in and move the enemy out. In order to do this effectively, we must grasp the necessity of divers tongues in establishing the Kingdom of Heaven.

> *Again, the kingdom of heaven is like unto a net, that was cast into the sea, and gathered of every* **kind** *[genos]: [48] Which, when it was full, they drew to shore, and sat down, and gathered the good into vessels, but cast the bad away.*
> *Matthew 13:47-48*

As the Kingdom of Heaven is likened to a net, divers tongues is the thread of the net. Each strand comprises a speaking, declaring or praying that will yield a tremendous harvest on this earth. As we speak in these Kingdom languages, we need to also ask God for interpretation. The Bible says, *"Wherefore let him that speaketh in an unknown tongue pray that he may interpret"* (1 Corinthians 14:13).

Interpreting the flow of what God is doing provides a marvelous opportunity to partner with Him. As in any type of fishing, the process of identifying what is caught and what should be kept for your current purposes is part of the enjoyment of the outing.

There are, it may be, so many **kinds** *(genos) of voices in the world, and none of them is without signification.*

1 Corinthians 14:10

God wants us to flow with Him in the vast depths of the Kingdom. We must understand that as we go deeper into the things of God, we require the ability to interpret what is being perceived.

The Enemy Utilizes Divers Capacities

Howbeit this **kind** *[genos] goeth not out but by prayer and fasting.*

Matthew 17:21

Here the enemy is shown to possess great diversity of operation. His holdings consist of areas and dimensions that were created by God and that the saints of the Lord are called to reclaim. There is a connection between *genos* and specific intercessory warfare.

In this verse, God shines His light on the existence of "multiple" domains of enemy operation. Through prayer and fasting, God will provide access points and an overcoming anointing that will serve to disarm and dismantle the strata of dark strongholds. We need a divers capacity to face a divers enemy. Our mode of victory is found through intensive fellowship with God within the framework of prayer and fasting. Such passionate devotion is fertile soil for a divers encounter of prayer. No matter who the enemy or what his weaponry, God will equip us with the Greater as we draw near in faith and devotion to His Purpose.

In Summary

We are a select group of people that have been adopted into the royal family and lineage of our Heavenly Father. Through our Lord and Savior, Jesus Christ, we can lay claim to the promised blessing of King David. Within that realm, we utilize many different languages and expressions to acquire and develop the Kingdom of Heaven. Part of this process is the identification of the enemy and his subsequent removal through anointed intercession.

When we combine the Scriptural references where *genos* is utilized, we perceive a clear picture of why God chose this word to define His gift of divers tongues.

Genos – a carefully selected word for a carefully selected purpose.

chapter 4

The Modern Day Church

The Prophet Speaks To Us

The Prophet Isaiah was a remarkable individual, and his anointed writings are very much alive today. He was gifted by the Lord to speak as a New Testament writer in a time that was centuries before Christ. What he says in regard to the modern church is nothing short of remarkable. How appropriate his insights, how needed his rebuke, and how vital his suggested remedies!

While the entire book of Isaiah is fantastic and well worth the read for every individual, let us look at Chapter 28 and focus on the need for the gift of tongues in our lives and in the Church. First, consider Isaiah's description of the modern church climate.

> *But they also have erred through wine, and through strong drink are out of the way; the priest and the prophet have erred through strong drink, they are swallowed up of wine, they are out of the way through strong drink; they err in vision, they stumble in judgment. [8] For all tables are full of vomit and filthiness, so that there is no place clean. [9] Whom shall he teach knowledge? and whom shall he make to understand doctrine? them that are weaned from the milk, and drawn from the breasts.*
> Isaiah 28:7-9

Success has made failures of many Godly men and many Godly movements. Typically, when there is a margin of prosperity, we are tempted to become as the parabolic individual who built bigger barns in order to house His good fortune. This misappropriation of blessing has always forged a gravestone for the Church. Quite literally, the modern church has become drunk on the wine of its past. It exists on reliving past experiences and crusades; however, grapes that were harvested in the last season can become quite intoxicating. This tragic state can render us unwilling to be apostolic in our pursuits.

Hebrews 6 admonishes the Church to be adventurous in God to the degree that we are willing to build upon our primary principles of doctrine and thought. We must all continue to be pioneers and not allow our last excursion to be the final frontier. To do this, the Scriptures say that we must leave the safety of our primary existence.

> *Therefore leaving the principles of the doctrine of Christ, let us go on unto perfection; not laying again the foundation of repentance from dead works, and of faith toward God, [2] Of the doctrine of baptisms, and of laying on of hands, and of resurrection of the dead, and of eternal judgment.*
> *Hebrews 6:1-2*

God is not interested in revival. He wants renewal of first passions, which only comes through wonder and expectancy. Romance involves finding new ways to communicate love. The heart of God longs for both faithfulness and creativity in our expressions of devotion to Him. He cannot long tolerate a contented church that abides in the tepid waters of lukewarm existence. He searches for those who cannot abide the thought of being anywhere other than where He is.

Precept Upon Precept

Where did we ever get the foolish notion that we have all the answers? Has anyone ever ascertained all of the counsel of God?

Isaiah 28:10 speaks of the necessity of adding precept to established precept and building line upon line. We must be willing to venture here a little to gain a new here, and there a little to claim another there. We must not become complacent. We must forge forward into present truth:

> *For precept must be upon precept, precept upon precept; line upon line, line upon line; here a little, and there a little.*
> Isaiah 28:10

This does not suppose that the old truths become invalid; however, we must press on toward higher ground. New revelation builds upon established foundation. Any other concept is unacceptable. Revelation is that new concept which was not conceived or imagined by the human mind. While we might accept a building upon whatever precept or line that is currently within our paradigm of thought or doctrine, it is the rejection of the "here a little and there a little" of God that often dooms us to mediocrity. Many people cite the verse, *"Eye hath not seen, nor ear heard, neither have entered into the heart of man, the things which God hath prepared for them that love him"* (1 Corinthians 2:9). However, when they see or hear something new, they reject it as not being of God. They want everything to line up with their traditions, their understandings and their experiences.

Unfortunately, when we speak of God doing a new thing, we are generally met with the upraised eyebrow of traditionalism. We must never get to the point where we feel that we are the bastion of *all* that God has ever revealed and of *all* that He ever will.

One of the wonders of our God is found in the knowledge that no matter what He has already done, He has something more beautiful to reveal. God is always doing a new thing, and our finite thinking cannot comprehend all that He has formed under the sun.

R And R

> *For with stammering lips and another tongue will he speak to this people. [12] To whom he said, This is the rest wherewith ye may cause the weary to rest; and this is the refreshing: yet they would not hear. [13] But the word of the LORD was unto them precept upon precept, precept upon precept; line upon line, line upon line; here a little, and there a little...*
> *Isaiah 28:11-13*

Isaiah speaks of "stammering lips and another tongue" that will yield revelation and understanding. This mode of enlightened pioneering will be empowered by God's promise of rest and refreshing.

We need the rest and refreshing because of the work of discovery, the stretch of application, and the warfare that withstands the opposition of the enemy. The "rest" that is associated with other tongues is the replenishing which comes from commune with our Father. He restores us and gives us a much-needed repair in the midst of our challenging tasks. The "refreshing" is the rejuvenation that propels us forward to face the task once more. Each of these essential elements comes through the process of speaking to our God in a tongue that is of His choosing.

We do not need the "rest" of the Lord in order to endure a sermon that has lasted five minutes longer than the allotted Sunday morning timeframe. Neither should we relegate this rest and refreshing of the Lord solely for usage in emergency situations. This is a mighty provision for those difficult times, but God wants His people to be proactive with His promise instead of adapting only a reactive stance.

Short Beds And Narrow Sheets

The word picture contained within Isaiah 28:20 is hard to miss and never fails to bring a smile to my face: *"For the bed is shorter than that a man can stretch himself on it: and the covering narrower than that he can wrap himself in it."* We have all faced the prospect of attempting to cover ourselves with a blanket that is just not large enough to do the job. We have probably also outgrown a bed or two in our lifetime.

Short beds and narrow sheets can only occur because of one thing – physical growth. In the natural, when physical growth and emotional growth do not coincide, we face problems. Whoever heard of a fifteen-year-old boy who has yet to move from his first crib? We would think that insane. As I was growing up, my mother would buy clothes for me that were always a little bit bigger than my current stature. While our earthly body is limited to a genetically predetermined size, our spiritual life should never cease to grow. Whenever we stop growing up, we begin to atrophy and the death process begins. This is true in both the physical and spiritual realm.

Shortened beds tell us that we will continually need to find *His* mode of rest. If we are praying in divers tongues, that rest will come in new and different ways but will always provide fulfillment. It is when we try to do God's work without sufficient prayer or when we are overly busied with our own interests that we face the shortened bed of unrest.

As the bed represents our growth and expansion, covering depicts what we put upon ourselves before the Lord. Let us consider some things that are implied when the subject of covering is addressed.

Covering represents our identity in God and His fellowship with us. When Adam lost his commune with God due to sin, he attempted to replace the coverage of God's glory with leaves. Covering serves to identify us as to our authority or place in the Kingdom. In the Old Testament mantles were given to prophets of great renown, and they not only identified the men of God but empowered them as well. In the New Covenant the Father gives robes of righteousness to honored sons. Covering also provides protection from the elements of the world. No matter what the terrain or climate, commensurate covering will be sufficient to counteract.

How often have we witnessed dying or out-of-touch ministries that once flowed in the power and dynamic of the Holy Spirit? This can occur for a number of reasons, but the greatest pitfall for any powerful ministry is failing to prayerfully seek God for fresh growth. Subsequently, the mantle that once covered them in grace and power is no longer sufficient for them.

God will often make things uncomfortable for you in order to move you into a larger realm of service to Him. You will either seek Him for the provision or try to maintain the momentum in your own flesh. Some people will even look for the insufficient and unsatisfying covering of the world. You must allow the Comforter to grow over you a fresh mantle of victory and provision. Yesterday's mantle is not sufficient for today.

God's Strange Ways

> *For the Lord shall rise up as in mount Perazim, he shall be wroth as in the valley of Gibeon, that he may do his work, his strange work; and bring to pass his act, his strange act.*
>
> *Isaiah 28:21*

A truism that I have heard is that God is under the amazing perception that *He* is God. What a thought! In order to become the people of God for any age, we must align with *Him*. We must allow *Him* to bring forth the new and the progressive. We must allow *His* strange ways and assume the wisdom of Gamaliel when he says...*"refrain from these men, and let them alone: for if this counsel or this work be of men, it will come to nought: But if it be of God, ye cannot overthrow it; lest haply ye be found even to fight against God"* (Acts 5:38-39). Any other position is a pretentious blight to our existence. The Spirit of God is life, and life is always vibrant and usually unpredictable.

Covenant With Death

If we delude ourselves into thinking that we have no need of God, a false sense of security comes, and we feel that we can elect to render ourselves neutral in the spirit realm. Whether we believe it or not, this world is a battle zone, and there are no neutral countries or individuals.

A large portion of the Church has attempted to make a covenant with death. Isaiah speaks about it:

> *Because ye have said, We have made a covenant with death, and with hell are we at agreement; when the overflowing scourge shall pass through, it shall not come unto us: for we have made lies our refuge, and under falsehood have we hid ourselves...*

> *[18] And your covenant with death shall be disannulled, and your agreement with hell shall not stand; when the overflowing scourge shall pass through, then ye shall be trodden down by it.*
>
> Isaiah 28:15, 18

There is no covenant with death. You will either be victorious in this life by virtue of fighting the good fight of faith or be conquered.

There is an unwritten code within much of the Church that simply says that we are holding on until the return of Jesus in the rapture. If we do not live that long, then we trust in the safety of the grave. This position forces us to cease living long before we are physically dead by unwittingly transacting an armistice with Satan. This uneasy truce states that we will leave him alone if he leaves us alone. We sing about power but never use it unless we are provoked or prodded.

Some champion the thought that "to stand" is the apex of faith, forgetting that the first admonition in this verse compels us to "do all."

> *Wherefore take unto you the whole armour of God, that ye may be able to withstand in the evil day, and having done all, to stand.*
>
> Ephesians 6:13

In order to do all, we must obtain a constant source of revelation and insight from our Heavenly Father. He longs to provide truth in this present hour.

chapter 5

A Need for Present Truth

A Climate Of Expectancy And Discovery

Why is it that Christians are so comfortable with finding a plateau and dwelling therein? The concepts of holding the fort and standing are essential dimensions of warfare, but they are lousy concepts for pioneering and discovery. A lack of crisp vision, fresh manna and present truth revelation has relegated the Church to the days of Eli the High Priest. We have become so accustomed to having *"no open vision"* that we are afraid of new truths and our *"eyes wax dim."*

> *And the child Samuel ministered unto the Lord before Eli. And the word of the Lord was precious in those days; there was no open vision. [2] And it came to pass at that time, when Eli was laid down in his place, and his eyes began to wax dim, that he could not see; [3] And ere the lamp of God went out in the temple of the Lord, where the ark of God was, and Samuel was laid down to sleep;*
> 1 Samuel 3:1-3

The Church has, in essence, lain down in its place, and the lamp of God has gone out. We cannot become comfortable in our place of worship. We need to be like Samuel who answered, *"Here am I"* and *"Speak, Lord; for thy servant heareth."* If we do this, the Lord will come and stand in our midst.

> *And the Lord came, and stood, and called as at other times, Samuel, Samuel. Then Samuel answered, Speak; for thy servant heareth. [11] And the Lord said to Samuel, Behold, I will do a thing in Israel, at which both the ears of every one that heareth it shall tingle.*
> 1 Samuel 3:10-11

As Samuel applied himself to the new thing of God, he became the man of power that God intended:

> *And Samuel grew, and the Lord was with him, and did let none of his words fall to the ground.*
> 1 Samuel 3:19

We have no concept of how to gain new vision, and most of our words fall to the ground in a loud but powerless fashion.

A primary dimension of divers tongues is that it establishes a climate of expectancy and discovery. ***Glossalalia***, or unknown tongues, unlocks mystery and welcomes an interpretation of the present thought of the Spirit. The Scripture says that when a person prays in the spirit, he speaks mysteries:

> *For he that speaketh in an* **unknown** [glossalalia] *tongue speaketh not unto men, but unto God: for no man understandeth him; howbeit in the spirit he speaketh mysteries.*
> 1 Corinthians 14:2

The word for **mystery** in the Greek original is ***apokalupsis*** and has a simple, yet profound meaning: to take the lid off and look inside. God is uncovering understanding and is implementing the gifts of the Spirit that He has reserved for this hour. This is happening through a Spirit-driven pursuit of praying "mysteries" into our reality. Divers tongues will help us to discover and enhance our understanding of the purposes and plans of our Heavenly Father. A mystery ceases to be mysterious when a light of understanding shines upon it. God's purposes are revealed through a progressive unveiling of mysteries. Today's mystery is birthed, and it becomes tomorrow's stepping-stone.

Divers tongues is necessary as God has earmarked this hour for rapid revelation and development. Someone must intercede this into reality using a communicative tool of great precision and alacrity.

The Missing Gifts Of Pentecost

When we look at the Book of Joel, we see that the promise of the Father was comprised of more than just the gift of tongues.

> *And it shall come to pass afterward, that I will pour out my spirit upon all flesh; and your sons and your daughters shall prophesy, your old men shall dream dreams, your young men shall see visions:*
>
> *Joel 2:28*

In quoting this passage on the day of Pentecost, Peter reiterates the fact that dreams and visions accompany the gift of tongues within the promise of the Father. Why is it then that those who speak with tongues do not press further into the fullness of prophecy, dreams and visions? Clearly the

Father desires that we combine these aspects of His revelatory gifts. Dreams and visions speak very directly of insights and fresh revelation for the children of God. Prophecy brings these and other insights into our realm of understanding.

Visions and dreams recognize the possibility that God desires to speak to us in ways that bypass our cognitive abilities. Since the Spirit of God to our spirit activates these capacities, they can be received in the day and in the night. Inherent in the Pentecostal experience is this mighty aspect of dreaming. God loves to communicate with us in ways that we cannot anticipate and imagine. We must welcome the fresh flame of illumination to sit upon our head once again.

Agnosticostals

The Apostle Paul begins his most prolific address regarding spiritual gifts in a rather profound manner, *"Now concerning spiritual gifts, brethren, I would not have you ignorant"* (1 Corinthians 12:1). The Greek word for **ignorant** in this verse is *agnoeo*. This term means to be disinclined toward information or to ignore the existence of something.

Agnostics don't deny the existence of God; they simply say that they don't care whether there is a God or not. As Pentecostals we need to recognize that at any juncture of revelation we can become agnostic about what God is doing. Jesus spoke of the leaven of the Saducees and Pharisees and that we should beware of this yeast. The Saducees do not believe that God moves in the present day. The Pharisees said that God could move but only in their framework. Agnosticostals combine the two yeasts and say that God doesn't move in new ways, only according to and limited to their understanding.

This is dangerous thinking. Paul warned the Corinthians not to be ignorant in the realm of spiritual gifts as God would continue to do wonderful new things therein. Paul concludes his treatise on spiritual gifts by granting this warning: *"But if any man be **ignorant** [agnoeo], let him be **ignorant**"* (1 Corinthians 14:38). People who are determined to be agnosticostals will be that, no matter what God is doing. God help us to avoid this fallacy at all costs.

Another misguided position is that God has already won the battle so we have no need to fight or pioneer. We need only to refer to a verse regarding our enemy: *"Lest Satan should get an advantage of us: for we are not **ignorant** [agnoeo] of his devices"* (2 Corinthians 2:11). We cannot ignore the existence of the enemy's devices. Our enemy is very much alive. To say that he is not or that we should be oblivious to his dealings is tantamount to giving him a major advantage over us. Ignorance is not bliss.

There is perhaps no foe greater than a wounded one. As long as our enemy exists, we will have to deal with him. Scripture tells us, *"The kingdom of heaven suffereth violence, and the violent take it by force"* (Matthew 11:12). The violent must still take the Kingdom by force. We either become violent for the Lord or we suffer the violence of this world and the enemy of our souls. A transliteration of this passage is that the Kingdom of Heaven is being crowded upon. Quite literally, forces of the enemy are contesting positions. It is a positional battle. The people of God must assert the ways of God and insist on gaining the field, taking it back for the Lord. There is no peaceful coexistence with the enemy.

Becoming Established

God wants to speak to us today. It is imperative that we hear from Him and act upon what He would say to us about our life and surroundings. Whether it be for the purposes of commune with Him, transacting Kingdom business, conducting warfare on behalf of the Lord, or any other facet of Kingdom living, we must have current and present truth from our Heavenly Father.

> *Wherefore I will not be negligent to put you always in remembrance of these things, though ye know them, and be established in the present truth.*
> *2 Peter 1:12*

While yesterday's truth will always be valid, present truth is what God uses to establish us in the now. Establishment shows us where to plant, how to build, what to produce, when to improvise or adapt new policies, when to sell and when to move afresh. Establishing is God's method of growth and development, and it comes through present truth. Knowing these truths brings freedom to us, and implementing them brings success in this life.

chapter 6

A Current Conversion

We Must Be Changed

Invention comes by the realization of necessity. If we assume that we need nothing, we become as those who would *"have no changes"* and subsequently are destroyed. Many anointed individuals in the Word did not continue to be used by God because of their inability to transition into the newness of childlike faith and expectancy. David characterized this calamity:

> *God shall hear, and afflict them, even he that abideth of old. Selah. Because they have no changes, therefore they fear not God.*
> *Psalm 55:19*

When we become complacent in our existence, we cease to fear God. Subsequently, we will not tolerate change in our lives. No change is equated with not fearing God. What a dangerous reality!

David knew full well the tragedy of this existence. Even the man who had a heart that sought after God was deprived of his heart's desire because he would not change.

David And The Temple

Consider with me the poignant tale found in 1 Chronicles 28 of David's ultimate surrender in life. King David gathered all of his leaders together and declared that he could not build the Temple. During his declaration, he defined the intent of building a house for the Ark of the Covenant and providing a footstool for the Glory of God.

David spoke of the vision that he received from God for the dimensions of the building and the revelation regarding the Temple utensils. He outlined the desires of God with perfect precision. Then, by God's further instruction, he relegated this magnificent prospect to his son, Solomon. Why? Because he would not change from the anointed one that he had been into the anointed one that God required.

On the surface, David's assertion of disqualification seems harsh. After all, God had made him to be *"a man of war"* (1 Chronicles 28:3). In fact, that facet of anointing was what thrust him into prominence in the battle with Goliath. One might consider that God was uncaring to disallow David to fulfill his life's passion simply because of the way that He had previously moved through him.

The reality is that God is not a hard taskmaster. There is something more here than meets the eye. God wanted David to build the Temple, but not with yesterday's anointing. David learned this principle early on when he could not wear Saul's armor into battle with Goliath. Now David was not able to lay down the armor of past victory and fame that had become imbedded within his own character and identity. Although David won God's heart by seeking Him in a new way every morning, David had become what his anointing *was* to such a degree that God could not do a new thing in him. This same tragedy occurred in other great men of the Bible.

Moses At The Rock

What about Moses? God did not allow him to cross over into the promised land! Again, God is not uncaring. The whole issue came to a head at the rock.

> *And Moses lifted up his hand, and with his rod he smote the rock twice: and the water came out abundantly, and the congregation drank, and their beasts also. [12] And the Lord spake unto Moses and Aaron, Because ye believed me not, to sanctify me in the eyes of the children of Israel, therefore ye shall not bring this congregation into the land which I have given them.*
> Numbers 20:11-12

Moses was again before a rock, and the people were complaining about thirst. God gave Moses a command to *speak* to the rock, but Moses struck it twice and chastised the murmurers in the process. Wait a second! Did not God previously use Moses to quench the thirst of the people through striking a rock? Did not God regularly become angry with the murmurers during the course of the forty-year journey? Why would God be so seemingly harsh with Moses to deprive him of the promise? It is because Moses would not adapt to a new thing. God wanted Moses to be a man who would "speak" prophetically into the rock. This had always been an insecurity for Moses.

When the original call came from the Lord, Moses tried to decline the call because of speaking limitations. He stuttered and was unwilling to make a public spectacle of his disability.

God honored Moses' timidity and sent Aaron to be a spokesman at Moses' side. Moses subsequently relied on Aaron, but increasingly his staff became a sign of God's strength and security before the people. Moses' rod had served the Lord with mighty demonstrations of His power. Pharaoh's magicians were defeated by it, the Red Sea parted by it, and the water from the rock had come because of it. Seemingly, the "rod" was Moses. Or was it?

God now wanted to revisit the point of Moses' greatest weakness. He desired for Moses to trust Him in the one area that he felt least competent – his voice. Moses needed to lay down his rod of security and trust God in the new thing. He wanted to demonstrate that Moses could be a prophetic voice in the ultimate realization of His leadership, the conquest of the promised land.

God began Moses' ministry by telling him to remove his shoes at the burning bush. Now He was telling him to lay down the rod. Moses was still the friend of God. Nevertheless, God had to find another man who would trust the vocal giftings and be obedient to a "new way." Joshua was that leader, and Jericho would be his first demonstration of a prophetic voice in harmony with God's power.

Elijah At Mount Horeb

What about Elijah? Coming from the most powerful culmination of his earthly ministry to that point, Elijah found himself unwilling to surrender his past anointing. He had just defeated 850 demonic shamans in a brilliant public display of

God's dominion. Nevertheless, he was not able to transition from a point of solitary ministry into one that was inclusive of other men of valor.

So what did he do? He ran from Jezebel and resorted to a lonely place. Eventually God led him to Mount Horeb, and twice in 1 Kings 19 God asked Elijah the same question and gained the same wrong answer: *"What doeth thou here, Elijah?"* Elijah's retort: *"I, even I only, am left."* This had been Elijah's identity. He was alone before God. He gained notoriety in this demonstration of obedience. What precipitated his removal from the earth in a whirlwind of fire was that he could not understand that there were seven thousand others who were serving Jehovah.

Elisha and Jehu were in the ranks waiting to burst onto the scene of obedience to God. However, Elijah was overcome by the doleful mantle of solitude in service to the King of Kings. What had served him over and over again had now become his nemesis and doomed him for replacement.

Except We Be Converted

In Matthew 18:3 Jesus related these Old Testament themes in New Covenant language. He commanded His disciples that *"except they be converted, and become as little children,"* they would not enter into the Kingdom of Heaven. Mind you, these are his disciples, not a group of unrepentant Pharisees.

And Jesus spoke to Peter in Luke 22:32: *"But I have prayed for thee, that thy faith fail not: and when thou art converted, strengthen thy brethren."* He then prayed for Peter so that a conversion would result from the process of testing. Subsequently, Peter could move forward into a position of strengthening his brethren because of his conversion.

God is continually interested in bringing us to the point of childlikeness. He does not want us to become childish in behavior. However, to enter into His Kingdom, we must be ready to learn things in a new way, accept new challenges, and demonstrate the excitement of the discovery of partnering with Him in whatever way that He chooses. We must become as little children. Any area within us that prevents us from submitting ourselves to Him in this way must be converted.

Surgery

Also in Matthew, Jesus warned of those things in our lives that would keep us from succeeding in this process:

> *And if thy right eye offend thee, pluck it out, and cast it from thee: for it is profitable for thee that one of thy members should perish, and not that thy whole body should be cast into hell. [40] And if thy right hand offend thee, cut if off, and cast it from thee: for it is profitable for thee that one of thy members should perish, and not that thy whole body should be cast into hell.*
> Matthew 5:39-40

The right eye represents the prophetic vision. He tells us that if our right eye is hindering us, we need to get rid of it. How can the proven prophetic vision keep you from entering into the Kingdom? Prophets must have a combination of foundation and pioneering. There can be a tendency to always interpret new things through the eye of your past revelation. When you face a new challenge of growth, you must not expect God to relate things to you the same way that He did in the past.

He also warned that if our right hand holds us back, we need to cut it off. The right hand represents relational influences. Those who previously helped you as co-laborers in Christ can be a hindrance to your changing into the new person that God needs for this hour. Sometimes these powerful friends are threatened by the thought that you will not need them or love them anymore if you do things differently in ministry to the Lord. Sometimes their pride is attached to the way that they mentored and assisted you, and they perceive your changes as a rejection of them. We must not miss the new of the Lord, no matter how persuasive the emotional issue may become.

The right hand is also symbolic of our personal dexterity, how we have succeeded in the past and what we have become famous for doing. You cannot always rely on past personal strengths to guide you through what the Lord is currently doing in you. It could become your greatest hindrance. Conversion is an ongoing process of old things passing away and all things becoming new.

What significance should be placed on Jesus' reference to hell in Verse 40 of this passage? The word translated "hell" is actually a designation for Gehenna, which was a valley outside the city walls that had been utilized to sacrifice children to demonic beings. In the days of Jesus' public ministry, it was a garbage dump wherein refuse was burned. In effect, Jesus was saying that we must stay current in our service to the King and in our battle against the enemy. Being cast into Gehenna would be much like discarded garbage.

In regard to wineskins, Jesus said that the old ones could not be entrusted with new wine.

> *And no man putteth new wine into old bottles; else the new wine will burst the bottles, and be spilled, and the bottles shall perish.*
> Luke 5:37

In regard to fruit production, he said that those branches that do not produce will be taken away.

> *Every branch in me that beareth not fruit he taketh away: and every branch that beareth fruit, he purgeth it, that it may bring forth more fruit.*
> John 15:2

We have been characterized by the Lord as the salt of the earth. He declares a sad end to salt that has lost its savor.

> *Ye are the salt of the earth: but if the salt have lost his savour, wherewith shall it be salted? it is thenceforth good for nothing, but to be cast out, and to be trodden under foot of men.*
> Matthew 5:13

Let it never be said of any true believer that the days of their effectiveness have come to an end. We must purpose within ourselves to always be of use to our Master.

What Shall We Then Do?

Complacency is a death sentence. We must be hungry for the righteousness of God and never become complacently satisfied with our yesterdays. Paul said that we should *"forget those things that are behind and reach forth unto those things which are before"* (Philippians 3:13). We must reach forth and embrace what God is bringing, and God is always bringing change.

Paul shared this principle with the Corinthian church:

> *But we all, with open face beholding as in a glass the glory of the Lord, are* **changed** [metamorphoo] *into the same image from glory to glory, even as by the Spirit of the Lord.*
> 2 Corinthians 3:18

Our changing, or "morphing," is God's requirement and is accomplished with His power. However, this process is not as easy as we might think because most of us are not willing to change. Even though the glory that transformed us into what we have become is both cherished and fantastic, God says that we must be willing to allow that same glory to change us again and again. Morphing is being changed into something other than what we are.

So what are some obstacles to this change? Pride? Perhaps. Ignorance? Definitely. Weariness of the cost involved? Undoubtedly. Nevertheless, we must be willing to let God change us and not stop short of receiving the fullness of God's power for our lives.

A Current Conversion

What Does All Of This Have To Do With Divers Tongues?

Great question!!!

If you are unwilling to change, divers tongues is not for you. If you are unwilling to serve as a champion for God, divers tongues is not for you. But if you are wanting all that God has for you and are willing to be what He created you to be in this hour, allow Him to grant this communicative gifting to you and it will revolutionize your life.

Our vile enemy will have a difficult time defeating those equipped with this modern weaponry from God. The forces of hell will be no match for the fire of a fresh Holy Spirit baptism. Imagine the confusion of the enemy defenses as God changes your language several times during a prayer session. Divers tongues changes you from reactive to proactive in a nuclear manner. The development of this Scriptural gift will enable you to step into a new type of prayer encounter that God desires, both individually and corporately.

God needs warriors that will champion His cause on this earth and in the heavenlies. Join the ranks!

chapter 7

Most Holy Faith

The Wisdom of Jude

The Canonical location of the Book of Jude is not without great significance, as the Holy Ghost strategically placed it as a precursor to the Book of Revelation. While Jude consists of a relatively small amount of verses, each of them is extremely potent.

Within this text, we discover a brilliant pattern for the preparation of the saints in the time of the end. Praying in the Spirit is essential to the process of ascertaining the purpose of God, as well as effecting the empowerment of His plan. In Jude 20, we find the declaration of a magnificent concept: *"But ye, beloved, building up yourselves on your most holy faith, praying in the Holy Ghost."*

Building A Most Holy Faith

"Building up" is a phrase with which we are familiar in the Scriptures. It means that we are progressively forming something. Bit by bit, we are constructing and developing. This sounds remarkably similar to what we discovered in Isaiah 28:10 regarding the *"line upon line, precept upon precept"* principle.

Here in Jude 20 we are not necessarily discussing the revelation of a mystery or a new truth. Rather, we recognize that this building is in reference to our most holy faith.

Praying In The Spirit — Not With Spirit

To pray in the Spirit is not synonymous with praying with passion, although passion is readily involved. Praying in the Spirit is not praying fervently about something that we understand cognitively. This prayer must be led by God's Holy Spirit. It is empowered by Him and driven by Him toward a completed task. Literally, it is the act of partnering with God in prayer.

Faith Does Something

Since faith is acting on something that we have not seen yet believe, it should be apparent that our praying in the Spirit would be in regard to purposes that God has envisioned for us. These purposes remain largely unfulfilled. God has purposes for our surroundings that will not be realized unless we align with Him. <u>The alignment begins to be instigated and instituted as we pray in the Spirit</u>. This is the impetus that God uses to turn our lives around as the Holy Ghost leads and guides us into *all* truth.

The "most holy" part of our faith refers to the ultimate purpose that God has in store for us. Sadly, most believers in Christ have not grasped that reality and live far below their privilege in Him. God speaks in Hebrews 5:12 about those who are babes, addicted to milk, refusing to grow into the meat of relationship with Him. These babies will not build anything that is "most holy" in their lives. In the New

Testament, God also tells us that there are many levels of authority in Him. Galatians 4:1 tells of some people that remain servants, though children of God. Romans 8:17 speaks of others who progress to become heirs but fail to move forward into the capacity of joint-heirs with Christ.

For most of the Church, a complacent abiding in the general faith precludes a progression into the walk and dominion of the saints. A more exhaustive discussion of this vital topic is available in the book entitled **The Saints**[1]; but for the purposes of our discussion, we need to understand a couple of essential terms. *Hagios* in the Greek language of the New Testament is regularly translated as both **saint** and **holy**. Holiness is not solely comprised of the task of avoiding sin or sinful actions. Holiness is a pursuit of the fullness of God. Those who pursue God's person and presence and allow Him to captivate their lives are literally "holies" or "saints."

The Holy Spirit is quite literally a saintly life or breath. He becomes the impetus or life force compelling us into a walk that is not ours, but God's. When we pray in the Spirit, we are interceding for God's ultimate purpose to be achieved within and through us. The "most holy faith" is, therefore, the building of the ultimate purpose of God within us – becoming like Him.

---

[1] **The Saints** by Ron Crawford, Pneumatikos Publishing

Holiness

Often, when holiness has been preached in the Christian world, it is in the vein of things that we cannot do – a list of don'ts. The enemy insists that holiness is a set of distasteful restrictions, even to the sight of many believers. However, holiness is not a restrictive influence in a negative sense. Rather, it is a proactive flow from the throne of God. To be holy is to be passionately in pursuit of God to the degree that things of this world are no longer appealing. After all, what on the earth compares to Him? Only those who have found this truth actually begin the process toward holiness.

Holiness is truly the process of pursuing and becoming what God made us to be. It is the fulfillment of all that God has planned for us and His power and presence in our lives. Holiness is not to be avoided but should be passionately desired and grasped. "Most holy" is the pursuit of the ultimate in our lives.

Back To Prayer

We return to the fact that this process will only develop as we pray in the Spirit. The Bible does not say that this process will build by virtue of our studying more, attending another seminar or having hands laid upon us in prayer. This development cannot be imparted. We must pray in the Spirit and, as we do, allow for the ultimate manifestation of this spiritual gifting – divers tongues.

chapter 8

Divers Intercession

Not Unto Men, But Unto God

The Scripture tells us in 1 Corinthians 14:2 that *"he that speaketh in an unknown tongue speaketh not unto men, but unto God: for no man understandeth him; howbeit in the spirit he speaketh mysteries."* What does that really mean? Some might read this verse and feel that it invalidates the concept of tongues as a tool for agreement and ministry to other members of the Body of Christ. It would be helpful to view other passages of Scripture that speak of ministry unto God and then glean the meaning of this passage about tongues.

1 Corinthians 10:31 pronounces, *"...whatsoever ye do, do all to the glory of God."* How about Jesus' own words in Matthew 25:40 where he proclaims *"...inasmuch as ye have done it unto one of the least of these, my brethren, ye have done it unto me"*? Or what of Matthew 25:43, *"I was a stranger, and ye took me not in: naked, and ye clothed me not: sick, and in prison, and ye visited me not"*? These verses speak of conducting ministry to and with people, but the ministry itself is actually being done unto God.

When we *"speak unto God"* in this light, we minister to men and women by virtue of the Scriptures cited above. As we utilize tongues in ministry, we are doing it unto Him. Saying that we speak unto God and not unto men also implies a relegation that commits what we say to the usage of the Lord. In this regard, we do not proceed with our own words. We also do not rely on anything other than His prerogative and directive in ministry.

Not Unto Men, But On Behalf Of Men

When the day of Pentecost was fully come in Acts 2, the gift and the office of divers tongues was birthed. Verses 8 to 11 list at least 15 different nationalities, each with a distinct language. Yet those hearing the disciples marvelled saying, *"And how hear we every man in our own tongue, wherein we were born?"* (Acts 2:8). We need to believe for the regular probability that we will be able to speak to people in their own languages *"the wonderful works of God."* That was and is Pentecost. The gift of divers tongues is to be used in points of ministry that we have traditionally relegated to obscurity and/or improbability.

If Two Of You Shall Agree On Earth

When interceding with someone else or when ministering to another person, divers tongues are extraordinarily useful. It is remarkable what can be accomplished when we are agreeing together in unknown tongues. However, when the Spirit grants the ability to pray in tandem utilizing the *same* unknown language, breakthrough occurs in a dynamic manner.

There have also been multiple times when intercessors in our church have linked with other bands of intercessors throughout the globe. It is nothing short of fantastic to be part of a group praying in an African dialect or another recognizable language. The welcoming of this cooperative gift is liberating individually and intensely powerful and effective.

Exact Prayers Before The Throne

The Father, Son and Holy Ghost are united in intercession toward our realizing the fullness of our saintly calling. Consider the Scriptures that teach us what occurs before the Throne of God:

The thoughts and voice of the Heavenly Father are expressed regarding our purpose and His plan (Revelation 21:5);

The intercession of Jesus on behalf of the saints (Romans 8:34, Hebrews 7:25);

The angels are given commands and reports flow between them and the Father (1 Kings 22:19-22; 2 Chronicles 18:18-21);

The intercession of all believers from across the planet (1 Kings 8:45,49; 2 Chronicles 30:27; Romans 8:14-17, 26-30; Hebrews 4:16; Revelation 8:3-4);

The accusation by the enemy and his minions against the saints (Job 1:6-12, 2:1-6; Revelation 12:10).

All of this and more occurs before the Throne of God. We are included in this intercessory appointment when we pray in tongues. Why have we relegated our prayers and the empowerment of the Spirit to earthly endeavor and pursuit? As the gift of tongues is an upgrade from prayer with the understanding, divers tongues is an upgrade from the level of unknown tongues. When divers tongues is applied, we are not limited by our own understanding or an individual prayer language. We are capable of morphing into any nuance or expression of the Spirit's choosing.

Groanings

> *Likewise the Spirit also helpeth our infirmities: for we know not what we should pray for as we ought: but the Spirit itself maketh intercession for us with groanings which cannot be uttered.*
> *Romans 8:26*

Groanings are a divers capacity of the highest order. I will never forget the times that God prayed through me in this distinct manner. It was truly an indescribable experience. Not only do you not have any conception of what is being vocalized, but also the way it is expressed is uncontrollable.

At the conclusion of one of our evening services, the Spirit of God descended in a glorious fashion. Immediately, people began to earnestly seek God's heart. Before I could decide what I intended to do as a response to God's visitation, I found myself on my face before the Lord. Not only did I lose my discretion as to posture, I also lost it in regard to vocalization. In other words, God did not care how I looked or sounded. My voice began to utter cries and bellows that emanated from deep within the diaphragm of my spirit. I looked strange and sounded even stranger than I appeared.

But I did not care about these things because I knew that God was moving through me in a manner of His choosing.

For the next half hour, this was my condition. Randomly, I could hear that other people in my congregation were experiencing the same thing. The same type of vocal expression was being uttered around the room. Words cannot define how it felt, where it came from, or what it meant.

As the visitation was lifting, I remember feeling how deeply I wanted for it to continue. There is simply no substitute for the feeling that comes from this type of commune with the Heavenly Father.

Body Language

We readily accept that "body language" is a real facet of communication. In fact, specialists in this field attest to the reality that communication from the body constitutes over 75% of the message. God speaks throughout the Scriptures of our entire body being used in devotional response to Him. Lifting the hands, laying prostrate, clapping our hands, shaking, and dancing are just some of these demonstrations. In intercession God will utilize our body in communicative ways that are sometimes unremarkable, sometimes beautiful and other times bizarre. Many critics have pointed to this body language as proof that God is not part of a particular outpouring. God says that our body is to be the Temple of the Holy Ghost, and He desires to use His Temple for intercession. Our physical body should be called a House of Prayer.

chapter 9

A Different Kind Of Prayer Meeting

Seek First The Kingdom

The beauty of divers tongues is that when we come together to intercede in this dimension, the Holy Spirit takes over. We are not praying for our will to be done, we are praying for God's will to be done. Truly, within this gifting we are seeking first the Kingdom of God and His righteousness.

God is well pleased with His people coming together for the purposes of serving His Kingdom and His will rather than for the purposes of airing our own individual requests. Too often we come together for prayer in church circles and spend more time citing prayer requests than in actual intercession. What a concept – praying as a service to God as opposed to a request session for our benefit.

God promises to meet our needs, but in Matthew 6:33, His order of seeking states that *"all these things"* will be added *only* after we seek Him and His will. Romans 8:28 says, *"And we know that all things work together for good to them that love God, to them who are called according to his purpose."* Notice that it says *His* purpose and not our purpose.

When I was elected as Pastor of our church, I was privileged to sit and talk with a respected pastor of a prominent Dallas church. He gave me wise counsel as to what he would and would not do if he were in my position as a young minister. After a number of minutes, he looked solemnly at me and shared with me his one regret in ministry was that he could not get his people to pray. He told me that his church could gather a crowd for anything other than a prayer meeting. I appreciated his genuine comments to me. Those words proved to be the most telling of any that I heard on that day.

For many years, my personal attempts to assemble people to pray were met with a placid response. A few diehards would join with me during announced intercessory times. Generally, I could count on people coming to pray either when they were in trouble or when someone near to them was struggling with a great need.

When my staff and I returned from Brownsville, we began to meet for prayer several hours every morning as well as a corporate time of prayer every Saturday evening. It was at this time that we first exercised the gift of divers tongues in intercession. Within weeks, a few intercessors joined us and also began to speak in divers tongues. The intercession was intense. It was as if we were fighting for the very life of our church.

Then, in January of 1997, we chartered a bus and took 56 members of our congregation to experience the Brownsville Revival. Everyone was very excited about what God was doing there but did not know what to expect. The Lord moved mightily and most were changed and returned with a greater hunger to seek Him. We felt the impartation was so significant to our Body that throughout 1997 we returned to Brownsville with different groupings, and the fire and passion in our worship services increased exponentially. There was an excitement and expectancy for what God might do in our church.

As time passed, however, I found out how little our general congregation actually knew about communing with God. Many of our people displayed a hunger for the Lord and followed hard after Him, but the longer worship services and the focus on prayer began to be wearisome for others. While many were seeking the Lord with abandon, others didn't really know how to relate to such a fervent climate. It was as if they wanted to be in the atmosphere of prayer, but their busy minds would find something else to do other than pray. Some would come just to talk with one another. Those who were only familiar with "emergency room praying" were desirous of finding someone for whom they could assist in "praying through" to victory.

Several became offended because, in their opinion, intercessors were more interested in seeking God than in helping each other. Many grew weary of waiting on God and of having their pastors waiting on God. They had grown accustomed to their personal issues and problems being center-stage instead of seeking first the Kingdom of God. Those who truly sought the Lord and dedicated themselves to intercession often found themselves accused by ones who were offended because they deemed themselves excluded. Generally, the accusations of these people stemmed from insecurities in their own lives, a competitive or jealous nature, or a very real opposition from the enemy. Sometimes all three elements existed in tandem. The truth is, most thought the refreshing was great, but it was time to go back to the way things were: cool, calm and collected. Sadly, these issues served to separate good people from the moving of God.

Make no mistake about it, though. God was and is moving! Transition occurred to such a degree that today we are a finely knit unified remnant that is willing to seek first the Kingdom of God at all costs.

Date Night With The Father

I asked the Lord how He would define our prayer times with Him. He simply said that they should be a time of heartfelt love and romance toward Him. We should be prepared to go anywhere He wants and have no agenda other than to be with Him. My labeling of this was simply "Date Night with the Father." While this might sound contrived to some, it truly is the best portrayal possible. This initially described our Saturday evening prayer meetings, but it became the motto for all of our corporate times before His Throne. As each person comes to intercede with a deep desire to meet with the Father, there is abandonment to His purpose. There is a freedom that comes when we simply devote ourselves to Him.

Typically after having inserted two or three current worship CDs into the sound system, our people converge to every part of our sanctuary. Some begin to dance before the Lord. Others stand with their arms extended toward the Lord. There are many who will prostrate themselves before God's face, and some that walk in intercession as did Enoch.

Whether we sing in the Spirit or declare openly in divers tongues, the Holy Ghost directs the flow of our ecstatic expression to the Father. God regularly orchestrates the dynamics of the prayer gathering, moderating the overall theme with great precision and detail. Often the room will hush in His presence only to erupt moments later in unexpected enthusiasm.

The key to the entire process is that God loves for us to seek after His heart. So few of His children seek Him for the sole purpose of knowing Him and spending time with Him. We were created for this privilege, and with great longing we look forward to our times of romance with our Heavenly Father. There is no formal beginning and no summation, as the passion of the encounter will define our course of action. God is a fantastic lover.

Getting Ready

Also, when our church gathers for intercession, our encounters with God are filled with a vibrancy of revelation. This requires a fluidity of movement and a flexibility of spirit. In essence, we never know what God is going to do. Rarely does He allow for advance notice as to His plans for a particular gathering so we've got to be ready.

When discussing this reality of corporate intercession, we pre-suppose that our intercessors have already done certain things before they arrive. First and foremost, it is vital that every intercessor is active in their personal time of commune with the Lord. Second, intercessors should not come needing to be cleansed from unconfessed sin. Coming to the church for corporate prayer without already being cleansed and "prayed up" is akin to reporting to the workplace without first grooming and dressing for the day. Third, personal issues, agendas and burdens should not be brought into a corporate setting of divers tongues.

In our church, we have a prayer room that is designed for individual pursuit of the Lord. We also have a chapel that is adjacent to our sanctuary in which we encourage everyone to check for "clean hands and a pure heart" before entering into a corporate encounter. Even with those two provisions, we continually have to remind people to be prayed up and prayed through before entering a corporate encounter. Further, the intercessor should be equipped with the whole armor of God according to Ephesians 6 and should be ready to receive additional spiritual weapons of God's choosing.

There are a few practical observations that need to be offered that will help us to enter in more gracefully and effectively. Hopefully, these bits of acquired wisdom will ward off predictable difficulties.

Common Diversions

Sometimes when we initially enter the sanctuary, there is a deep spiritual climate into which we have not yet become acclimated. No matter how many depths we have been privileged to experience in God, there is always something more that we have not yet encountered.

When people with varied anointings come together, the synergy of their giftings and the ***rhema*[2]** of the moment combine to create something fascinatingly new in the Lord. When we come upon a climactic engagement such as this, there are some responsibilities and rules of order that must be observed.

We have to respect the fact that God has ordered our steps and know that we have not missed out on anything in which we were supposed to be involved. We cannot be anointing chasers, we must not entertain undue curiosity, and we must avoid jealousy with all of our might. Our response must be to find a place to ask the Lord what He wants us to do and to ascertain that directive. We have to know that sometimes God desires for us to join a breakthrough point in the line of battle; while at other times, we must hold the flank as others breakthrough. The children of *Zebulun* were commended for their military prowess because they knew how to keep rank (1 Chronicles 12:33).

It is often tempting to rush to the flashpoint of what God is doing. Sometimes God desires for us to join with those who are experiencing a powerful breakthrough, but this is not always the rule. Our sensitivity to the direction of our Commander regarding what *we* are to do in response to what *He* is doing in our midst is very important.

---

[2] ***Rhema*** - A timely word for the present hour

Watchers And Watchmen

One of the most distracting things that can occur during a divers encounter is to have onlookers in the midst. Sometimes when our intercessors are deep in prayer or a particularly unique prophetic demonstration is happening, I will notice individuals who are simply watching. At times, we all watch to witness what God is doing. Whenever it is done in appreciation or with an eye toward coordinated participation, watching is acceptable.

Watchers that are simply onlookers are another matter entirely. Typically, they are novices and have no earthly idea what is going on. Watching in this case will not engender anything good. The insecure or competitive person will even be prone to jealousies or emulation, and neither of these is acceptable in any measure.

On the other hand, God will use individuals, like watchmen of old, who will sense particular incursion points of the enemy. These people are mobilized by the Father to stand in the gap for a particular prayer meeting. The Lord says in the Word that He seeks for an intercessor for this purpose. Generally, these will be seasoned members of the established team of intercessors within the house.

> *And I sought for a man among them, that should make up the hedge, and stand in the gap before me for the land...*
> *Ezekiel 22:30*

The gap is a place in the camp or wall where the enemy will seek to pour through the defenses. God needs for people to stand there and defend the intercessory assignment. Like Nehemiah who rebuilt the wall, some need to build while others watch in defense.

In Matthew 6, the Word tells us that in our alms service and in our prayer times before the Father, we need to have as our prime motivation the goal of worshipping the Father. However, it is a rare day that the Father does not have something for us to do. We never know how we might be used. Our experience has been that one hand of the intercessors are doing the primary function of creation or acquisition of the spiritual purpose of God while the other hand is taking care of a less visible but necessary watchmen and support function. To those who are on the left hand, the Lord says they do not need to be concerned with what the right hand is doing. That function is not for them to know or be intimately acquainted with at that point of service.

Watchers are fine if it is for the temporary aim of ascertaining the call of the Lord for their ministry. Watchmen are essential for guarding the camp in their ministry before the Lord.

A great rule of operation is also a simple rule. When in doubt as to what you should be doing in a prayer gathering, press into the Lord with all of your heart. Keep your eyes on Him and not on other people. Perceive the encounter with the eyes of your heart and not your head. The key is to seek the Lord and not the experience – no matter what is transpiring around you.

Needs, Urgencies And Emergencies

Often there have been "emergencies" that have arisen prior to or during prayer times. Soon, many who have essential intercessory assignments before the Lord are drawn away to attend to this crisis or that necessity. The enemy hates intercessory divers tongues.

We have undoubtedly been around a child that displays no concern for his surroundings or for protocol. The needs of that child become his only focus and the acquisition of attention his only pursuit. Overprotective guardians are equally to blame in causing distraction while attending to the demanding little one. The Church is filled with both spiritual babies and overprotective guardians. For divers prayer to work, these two groups must be trained. Unquestionably, this is an issue of spiritual understanding and maturity, and there is perhaps no greater enemy to a divers encounter than this issue.

We are warned in the Word of God that there are many who are not weaned from milk (Hebrews 5:12). Some are sustained by milk because they are legitimately babes; others remain babes by choice. For the Apostle Paul, this type of hindrance was a great source of personal dilemma, and it abides today as an ongoing challenge for the Church.

Legitimate emergencies are a different type of diversion. We must be trained and drilled in military fashion for these situations as well. We must know how to hold our ground, maintain position, and remain vigilant in the watch no matter what is happening around us or to whom it is happening. Someone will need to be responsible to handle emergencies when they arise during a battle. The other warriors need to trust that the situation is being lovingly cared for until the Lord is finished with the foray of the hour. It does not take much diversion to impede the momentum of battle.

Authority

Established authority is always necessary in a divers prayer session. In other words, there needs to be a recognized leader. Some will brand this a control issue. I counter with the fact that where there is no recognized authority, the enemy will appoint one.

In our church, we do not expect the pastor to be the security force of the meeting. Like Nehemiah, the spiritual leader should not be constrained to come down from the wall in order to rectify interpersonal issues. Instead, we utilize a designated security group, as well as a team of trained Prayer Captains.

The security group will be on the lookout for the occasional intruder that has an agenda other than prayer and Godly pursuit. The Prayer Captains will serve to supervise the general conduct of the meeting. This may appear restrictive, but I assure you, it is necessary. If something similar to this is not in place, the divers meeting will likely be interrupted over and over again. Subsequently, the spiritual leaders will continually be diverted from their necessary pursuit of the Lord. Many types of people, some well-meaning and others not, can become a hindrance to divers prayer if they are allowed the chance. This is not an elitist viewpoint. It is one born of experience. The desire of the enemy is to stop the meeting altogether, and these are the avenues that he employs.

In Matthew 18:19, the Lord speaks of agreement in prayer between two believers. The Greek word for **agree** is *sumphoneo*, which is the root of our English word for symphony. Every symphony must have a conductor. With no conductor, virtuosos will abound or sections will emphasize their own priority. The key point of this warning is that God needs to be in control, and He will flow in a divinely ordered structure. Divers intercessory gatherings will not function properly if individuals are allowed to set the agenda, whether by design or emergency. There is a very fine line here between control and guidance. Yet, I state definitively that spiritual environments demand authority structures; otherwise, the sheep will find a way to wander aimlessly or the enemy will drive them where they don't belong.

Divers Tongues

chapter 10

A Different Kind Of Intercessor

Timing Is Everything

Why is a gift like divers tongues being launched forth in this hour? Before the answer is offered, let us affirm that God has dynamic ways of highlighting the truths of His Word at crucial junctures in history.

For instance, why were the efficacies of the Word and the power of faith so prominently defined during the days of Martin Luther? After all, those truths have become the cardinal rules of order for the modern day church. They had always been in the Bible, but God chose that hour of emphasis in order to highlight and develop understanding of those truths. They now define the course of His people and the world.

What about the Pentecostal move that thrust forth at the beginning of the twentieth century? Wasn't Pentecost in the Bible before that time? Or, did God release a new emphasis and fresh anointing in that hour?

The past century has served to debut a steady timeline of ***rhema*** focuses from the Throne of God. Peter referred to this facet of God's work in the church as a "present truth." At the beginning of this new century, divers tongues is one emphasis that God has targeted for prominence.

A Global Language

Our world is becoming smaller, and agreement is being forged on a global scale. Nations are being unified by virtue of advances and availability in the computer and satellite industries. Truly, the days of Babel are upon us again. A one-world economy will soon be here. The last time this occurred on earth, God had some curious statements to make as He viewed the efforts of mankind.

Review Genesis 11 with me. God came down to a place called Babel and looked at the tower to the heavens that man was attempting to construct. The construction project was not problematic for the Most High, as man is always attempting to build something of great notoriety. The problem that God cited was the unified language as found in Verse 6:

> *And the Lord said, Behold, the people is one, and they have all one language; and this they begin to do: and now nothing will be restrained from them, which they have imagined to do.*
> *Genesis 11:6*

God defined the moment as one in which the people were in accord and that their unified language would allow them to do anything. Their imagination would flourish, and they would be restrained by nothing because of a commonly shared language. God did not destroy the tower. He did not hinder the building process itself and he did not afflict the leaders. He separated the language.

Once again, mankind comes together in unified fashion. In this hour, the circumstances are markedly different, and God has a markedly different answer, and it is God's time for overcoming. He is mobilizing His people and this is the battlefield of His choosing. What is His weapon of choice for this final conflict? His weapon is His unified voice to us, in us, and through us.

A Bigger Picture Than We Can Imagine

Human beings tend to view their world as an end in itself, and each generation feels that it is the apex of civilization. However, God's timeline is eternal and incredibly precise. Within that timeline, there are junction points of great importance. These significant moments touch each generation, and in each generation God looks for people that are willing to do His bidding.

Throughout the Scriptures, we see key individuals pinpointed by God in order to serve a divine purpose for that hour. His eyes are still searching *"to and fro throughout the whole earth."* He is looking for a partner to believe and follow His plan for this hour.

> *For the eyes of the Lord run to and fro throughout the whole earth, to shew himself strong in the behalf of them whose heart is perfect toward him.*
>
> 2 Chronicles 16:9a

Marveling And Wondering

Twice in the New Testament our Lord Jesus is described as marveling, and both times it was in regard to the faith of people. Once He marveled at belief and once He marveled at unbelief.

In the Old Testament, Isaiah 59:16 describes God as "wondering" or looking for a person who would be an intercessor. The Hebrew word for **intercessor** here is *paga*. *Paga* is a colorful Hebrew expression that lends itself to a wide and varied interpretation. Of the over forty usages in the Old Testament, it encompasses some of the most beloved passages and themes known to believers. Isaiah 53 uses this word twice to prophetically describe the intercession of Jesus. The word *paga* always seems to be utilized by the Holy Spirit to depict the mandate of God operating through a person.

God is "wondering" again today. He is wondering who will hear His voice and become a person that He can use to establish His powerful and progressive realities for this age. God is looking for those who will answer the call to be a *paga* for their city, nation and continent.

Place Of *Paga*

Wherever heaven touches earth, *paga* intercessors will be called upon by God. The patriarchs were continually raising altars to the Lord at points of unusual divine encounters on this earth. While every locale is important to God, there are some places that are more strategic than others. God is erecting communication centers of the Spirit on every continent, and He is manning these centers with *paga* intercessors.

When Moses was establishing the dimensions of the promised land in Numbers 34:11, he told the people that they needed to "reach unto," or *paga*, a border of God's choosing. Intercessors will establish outposts of prayer wherever they are assigned. From these locations, Kingdom business is conducted by God through His people.

Places are important to God. These outposts on earth represent specific junctures in the spirit realm. They are each unique, and God is uniquely equipping warrior intercessors to "light upon," reclaim and establish the purposes of the Heavenly Father within them. At these specific locations, angelic interaction will increase, and intercessors assigned to these locations will partner with angels in ways that have yet to be seen or heard. This topic will be covered in greater detail in Chapter 11.

Assignments given to intercessors will be of a heavenly nature. Plans of phenomenal significance will be revealed and established. There will be wrestling and refining. They will gain greater authority with every point of submission of their lives to Him. As God said to Jacob in Genesis 32, great favor will be granted before God and man. Authority is given as an extension of their saintly calling and responsibility.

People Of *Paga*

On various occasions, the word *paga* is attributed to the command and influence of a king or leader. Generally, these instances are declared as a means for the edicts of the throne to be applied.

Patriarchal Examples of Paga

Jacob had two *paga* encounters. In Genesis 28:11 he "lighted upon" Bethel and had an extraordinary encounter with the angels. God's portal was operative in that place, and Jacob called it the house of God.

Additionally, in Genesis 32:1, God's angels "met" Jacob at Mahanaim, the place of two armies or camps. Later in the same chapter, Jacob wrestled with God. His name was changed and he was declared to be a prince with God. Jacob was the covenant man of his day and hour. He was the one that God was using to establish principles and places. In both instances of his ministry, communication with God and His heavenly forces was paramount. God broke down the barrier between the earthly and the divine. There was no hindrance between Jacob and Himself.

Kingly Examples of Paga

Those who have been given authority in the land will need to rely heavily upon *paga* intercessors. God will assign these people to His anointed leaders. In the Old Testament, we have some dynamic and instructive examples of how people with a *paga* anointing were utilized by King Saul and King Solomon.

• King Saul and Doeg the Edomite

King Saul always seemed to be self-motivated rather than God-motivated. His goals were to please the people and to defend His borders and throne rather than to please God and expand the kingdom of Israel. In Saul's domain, the *paga* was utilized in a corruptive and evil manner. Saul's *paga* was an evil man named Doeg the Edomite. A descendant of Esau, Doeg possessed a generational anointing.

When Saul was attempting to assassinate David, the priests of the Lord at Nob rose to the aid of David. This infuriated Saul, and he sought to kill God's mediators. The only man who would accommodate the dastardly request was Doeg the Edomite. The horrid account of Doeg's "falling upon" eighty-five priests is found in 1 Samuel 22:18.

This was a terrible and egregious occurrence, but it displays a side of the *paga* that is true of all such who hold that designation. *Paga* intercessors will defend the king. In fact, they relish the thought and are willing to fulfill the duty with their entire livelihood. This is why it is imperative that we stay in line with God and commit ourselves to His present truth. We could be utilizing our God-given anointing in support of yesterday's move. In doing so, we attack the very thing that God holds dear and precious. Recurrently, the present move of God is most fervently attacked by the champions of His last move.

True worshippers, like the priests of Nob, will welcome the new anointing God is bringing. Those who are like Saul will defend their territory and attempt to please people rather than God. These individuals will be tempted to strike out against the progressiveness of the Lord. God, grant us wisdom to avoid this tragic miscalculation.

- **King Solomon and Benaiah**

King Solomon utilized a mighty man of renown named Benaiah as his *paga*. Benaiah was the captain of the host under King David, and he was also the leader of the Palace Guard. He was utterly devoted to the kings under which he served. He was commanded by Solomon to "fall upon" three men who were also mighty in position and stature. In doing so, Benaiah demonstrated three vital roles of the *paga* in regard to leadership.

***Paga* versus Insurrection:** The *paga* will react strongly to those who exalt themselves against leadership. Adonijah was one of David's sons not chosen to succeed his father on the throne of Israel. His maneuverings to upstage Solomon were sometimes clandestine and outrageous. When Solomon had experienced enough of this, he called upon Benaiah to "fall upon" Adonijah.

While the thought of killing someone is both immoral and unchristian, the concept of preserving proper authority in the modern church is valid. There will be less display of rebellion to authority within the house of the Lord if it is known that strong men and women of God will not tolerate such behavior. When a *paga* of the Lord is present, such rebellion will be rare.

***Paga* versus Self-Interest:** The second instance of Benaiah as a *paga* is found in 1 Kings 2:29. It involves Joab, the former commander of the army who had served faithfully under King David. While this is a long and involved story, some salient points are worth mentioning within the discussion of the *paga*.

Joab's downfall came because he disobeyed David's command and settled a personal issue by murdering Abner in recompense for killing his brother. David never forgot this injustice and made Solomon swear to eliminate Joab. When Solomon succeeded David to the throne, Joab further alienated himself by foolishly supporting Adonijah's quest for kingship. The combination of unwise decisions led to the necessity of Benaiah's *paga* ministry, and Joab was killed. Not even his appeal to the Horns of the Altar would serve to save his life. What a terrible end to a life committed to God's service!

To us, this episode in the Word can appear outrageous; but in the larger light of Scripture, it lends a telling lesson for all to see. There is no room for self-interest in the life of the believer, particularly when it conflicts with the expressed word and intent of spiritual leadership. Given a choice between our agenda and the established authority, God will uphold authority.

Benaiah and Joab were military contemporaries and had undoubtedly been comrades on the battlefield on numerous occasions. The *paga* will sometimes have to fulfill God's assignment at the cost of personal relationship. In the realm of the Spirit, authority is of paramount importance. The *paga* must enforce God's authority because obedience to the Lord's authority is the glue that holds intercessory structure in place.

Paga versus Impetuousness: 1 Kings 2:46 describes Benaiah's last recorded instance of serving the king in a *paga* role. A relative of the late King Saul named Shimei was openly contentious of the lineage of King David. The heartfelt discontent for leadership was displayed with his words and actions. On one occasion when David was fleeing from Jerusalem during a coup attempt by Absalom, Shimei cursed the king to his face in a very theatrical display of contempt (2 Samuel 16:13). While David turned the inexplicable insult into a demonstration of piety before the Lord, Shimei's actions and the feelings that prompted them were common knowledge among the people of God.

In light of the above, what Shimei ultimately did to prompt his death seems trite. Essentially, he left Jerusalem to retrieve a group of servants who had ran away. The problem with this reasonable action was that it was against the understood rule of King Solomon that Shimei remain in Jerusalem as a condition of his allegiance to the lineage of David. Shimei could have asked permission to retrieve his servants or he could have sent someone else to attend to the task. Instead, he acted on his own volition and abridged his agreement with the king. As a result, Benaiah was subsequently ordered to "fall upon" Shimei.

This point is significant spiritually. Sometimes, those who have a predilection for impetuous actions and damaging speech necessitate strict rules being placed on their behavior. This is not cruelty or unforgiveness, but wisdom. Talented and anointed people sometimes feel that they can say or do anything at anytime. Some have wrongly assumed that *paga* is some kind of wide-open, "anything goes" type of worship experience in the Lord. God never entertains an "anything goes" atmosphere. Instead, "everything goes" in accordance with His purpose and His business.

Anyone moving in the office of divers tongues will have to employ a bevy of Benaiahs. There will be constant challenges to authority and regular instances of willful disobedience. *Paga* intercessors are essential to maintaining order within the camp of the Lord. They are not to be heavy handed, but they cannot consent to rebellion.

God is looking for people to whom He can entrust His authority. Those who stand as a *paga* will need to stay in submission to leadership and be willing to stand with leadership in "falling upon" issues of God's choosing.

Paga Power

Paga is also utilized to depict the warfare of the Lord God Himself. In Isaiah 59:16, God accepts an active role as intercessory warrior:

And he saw that there was no man, and wondered that there was no **intercessor** [paga]*: therefore his arm brought salvation unto him; and his righteousness, it sustained him.*

Isaiah 59:16

If we are willing to commit to God in true devotion and intercession, God can show forth His mighty arm through us. He will establish His righteousness in this earth.

chapter 11

Of Men And Of Angels

Ministry In The Heavenlies

So often we focus our efforts and our conversations on mundane issues even though the Word clearly states that our conversation should be in the heavens. We must hearken to Philippians 3:20 which says, *"For our conversation is in heaven; from whence also we look for the Saviour, the Lord Jesus Christ."* We are to be seated NOW in the heavenlies, according to Ephesians 2:6: *"And hath raised us up together, and made us sit together in heavenly places in Christ Jesus."*

One of the attributes of divers tongues is that it enables us to minister with great fluency in the intercessory realms of the heavens. Many times, the Lord has communicated to and through the angelic host by virtue of this gift.

Ministers To The Heirs Of Salvation

The ministry of angels will be prominently apparent to those who are operating in a saintly capacity. Angels minister within the development and application of the heirs of the Lord God. An heir is a distinct designation. There is a great Scriptural difference between a believer and an heir.

> *Now I say, That the heir, as long as he is a child, differeth nothing from a servant, though he be lord of all;*
> *Galatians 4:1*

The writer of Hebrews speaks of this angelic assignment on behalf of the heirs of salvation.

> *Are they not all ministering spirits, sent forth to minister for them who shall be heirs of salvation?*
>
> Hebrews 1:14

These angels minister to those who determine to commit themselves to the purposes of the Father. They are not just guardian angels making sure God's children stay out of harm's way, although they do fulfill this protective function. The people who embark on the pathway of obedience to Him and His eternal business will be assisted by the heavenly host. This is what it means to move from the elemental levels of the Kingdom into the progression of developing as an heir and joint-heir in Christ.

Why Angelic Tongues?

Divers tongues allows the believer to pray in God's chosen language that best fits the intercessory need. Sometimes the language is an unlearned earthly tongue, often it is truly the language of angels. Some would ask why we would need to respond to an angel in a language other than our own. In my opinion, there are two valid reasons.

First, there are limitations to what our own languages are capable of conveying. In discussions between nationalities, each country feels that their language is most efficient. When God separated languages at Babel, it is quite likely that He removed some of the effectiveness within each of the languages. Secondly, there is the likelihood that our mind would not be able to fully verbalize the awesome nature of all that God wants to communicate. Angels deal with concise directives. They do not enjoy the latitude of interpreting what we mean or do not mean. Just as the Word tells us to judge prophecy and hold fast that which is good, we can deduce that our human ability to speak God's message is sometimes alloyed with our own perceptions.

The Apostle Paul chose His words under the direct inspiration of the Holy Ghost. The words were not written for the purpose of poetic flow. When he said, *"though I speak with the tongues of men and of angels"* (1 Corinthians 13:1), he was not euphemistically referring to the languages of heaven. Divers tongues will include the languages of earth, both extinct and current. They will also include the languages of angels.

Often the arrival of various angelic corps during one of our services or times of corporate prayer will be signaled by a variation of our prayer languages. When angels are in close proximity, there is a strong unction to speak in angelic tongues. You *cannot make this happen on your own*. The Holy Spirit is the director of every encounter. He is the One that anoints and activates you to interact with angels.

Angelic Languages

There are many different hosts of angels. God has defined them according to their duty and service to Him. Similar to the tribes of Israel, they have characteristics and responsibilities that mark them as distinct from each other. In this regard, it has been my experience that angels are multi-lingual in that they are able to converse in the language of the country or region to which they have been assigned as well as their native angelic tongue. I have observed that each of these designations have their own distinct dialect and dimension of communication. God is creative. If we have trouble with that concept, we need only to consider the complexities within the natural world in which we live. The same is true of the heavenly realm.

There are warring angels who form separate armies, angels of worship, angels who yield skill and understanding, and others that guard over mysteries in the heavens. Many angels dynamically minister before the Throne; others are like ambassadors serving as liaisons between the Throne room and other locations; some are guardians of the heavens; some are assigned to denominations; and others watch over the development of the saints in drill sergeant precision.

Some angels speak in eloquent dialogue while others have melodic voices. Some angels communicate with such speed that they almost buzz as they convey their assigned message while others methodically drone. There are those who sound like instruments and those that deliver resounding tones that rock the ear and heart alike. There are those who are gravely solemn and others who are jubilant.

Manner Of Commune

It is quite exhilarating to be permitted to communicate with angels. There have been times when we have been called to pray over certain lands and groups of people, and we have seen the angelic intervention which was empowered by virtue of this intercession.

At other times, the Lord allows us to worship Him in the company of a great gathering of angels. Our tongues and mannerisms vary according to the course of the winds of the Spirit. Angels love to worship the Father. When the seraphim are present, intercession and worship are especially explosive. They engender some of the most prolific and supernatural dances that I have ever witnessed. The Judah angels are triumphant in their expression. They yield an anointing of jubilant shouts and horn-like sounds that are accompanied by some of the most unusual and exuberant utterances that I have ever heard.

Whenever various armies of angels mobilize in our midst, dynamic and bold intercession occurs. Not only can there be several distinct languages in operation, but the Holy Spirit regularly organizes our people into various groupings in order to share in agreement within the particular dialects. The types of languages are awesome in precision and beauty and can change on a moment's notice.

From crescendo to decrescendo, God directs a divers prayer encounter as He would a symphony. When the angelic host are directly involved, it is nothing short of spectacular.

What Types Of Messages Do We Convey To Angels?

When God places us in a location of service, He gives us responsibility along with our authority. God assigns angelic teams to specific areas of responsibility. They serve as specialists to assist us in accomplishing His purposes for our lives as well as for the place to which He has assigned us.

The Father allows His sons to flow in authority with His angelic host in the liberation of this planet from the bondage of fallen angels. Adam fell because of a fallen angel. Now the descendants of Adam partner with the holy angels in restoring the earth to God's authority and rule.

As we intercede for a particular purpose to be accomplished, God not only intercedes through us but also uses us to communicate the plan of provision or attack to the angels that He assigns to accomplish that plan. Daniel is an example of such a man of prayer. Although he was an Old Testament saint without the benefit of Holy Spirit baptism, he nevertheless was utilized by God to prayerfully cooperate with angelic activity for the restoration of the homeland of God's people. Angels warred and conquered as a result of and in harmony with his intercession before God. The importance of divers tongues is that we do not have to know what we are praying as God is in total control.

Spiritual Authority

Angels respond to the authority of the Father and to the authority that He has given to His children here on earth. For those churches who recognize the call of Hebrews 12 and press on toward Mount Zion, there will be an innumerable company of angels present. The angelic will become so prevalent that often the congregants of such a church will *"entertain angels unawares."*

In our intercessory flow as an office of divers tongues and interpretation, the angelic forces of the Lord are continually among us. God's angels never come into our church without being respectful of and subject to the Father's established authority within that house.

Often when I visit another assembly of believers, I am presented to the angelic hierarchy within that house, and I submit myself to the Lord's authority therein. It is the enemy who disregards authority structure. We can generally tell whenever a prophet is in right standing with God by the way they respect the established authority structure within a church.

God's Kingdom is one of authority and respect for authority. Angels do not know any other way.

Divers Warfare

Dark angels contest whatever the Heavenly Father is doing, and we often battle against them in intercession as the Lord directs. They do not want to surrender dominion; and therefore, they contest the incursion of God's conquering armies.

Sometimes during intercession, the Lord will give us insight into the enemy realm. It is helpful to interpret what the other side is declaring and fearing. This topic must be met with obedience and divine wisdom and not a cavalier attitude.

Once, after being given a particular intercessory assignment by the Lord, I was confronted by a powerful and belligerent demonic being. This being was intent on contesting my authority to do what God had commanded and would not yield. Suddenly my tongue changed into a dialect that was different from any that I had previously encountered. The look on the face of my foe altered in a bizarre manner. He stepped back and vanished.

As I inquired of the Lord about this, God impressed me that He had given me access to a language that this being had utilized before the fall. My unexpected usage of this language befuddled the enemy and his outward demeanor became deflated. It was apparent to me that he was embarrassed by the entire episode. The interpretation of the message was something from the Father directly to this being. The best that I could ascertain from the conversation began with God calling this being by its proper name and went something like this. "You know that I have given my servant authority, so why are you not yielding? I stand behind the word that I am speaking through him. Hearken to the directives through my servant or contend directly with me. You choose."

Cautions

Of course, only the Lord God Almighty can order this type of meeting. It must not be dabbled in or sought after, and it definitely is not for the weekend warrior. God is looking for joint-heirs. He will not entrust higher giftings as novelties but only as life callings to committed warriors.

For a more complete discussion of this topic, please obtain a copy of the book, **Ministering With Angels**[3].

---

[3] **Ministering With Angels** by Paul David Harrison, Pneumatikos Publishing

chapter 12

A Different Kind Of Warfare

Partnering With The Father

Prayer has been miscast in most of the church world. For many, the topic of prayer is boring. For others, it becomes the shtick of their individual piety. To some, prayer is a last-resort plea before the court of heaven in a final attempt to be bailed out of a real and present calamity. Invariably, prayer is relegated to the concept of presenting a need or wish list before the Father. What a wearying and unpleasant prospect. This misguided application of communication with God is a tragic distortion of what prayer really is and should be.

Prayer is communing with the Heavenly Father and ultimately partnering with Him. We were created both for the purposes of communing with Him and for partnering with Him, but we generally do not come into alignment with the reality of God's ongoing plans for us and for where He has placed us. This communing prayer is perhaps the greatest target of the enemy. Satan and his cohorts will fight against the true institution of prayer and communication with God. He has assigned his frontline troops to ensure that prayer does not become what it was designed to be, thereby hindering God's purposes which those prayers are designed to accomplish.

The Mandate Of Jesus

> *And these signs shall follow them that believe; In my name shall they cast out devils; they shall speak with new tongues; [18] They shall take up serpents; and if they drink any deadly thing, it shall not hurt them; they shall lay hands on the sick, and they shall recover.*
>
> Mark 16:17,18

There is perhaps no passage in the Word of God that has been more maligned than the one cited above. Biblical critics have assailed this as not being worthy to be included in the Canon of Scripture. Their reasons are numerous but unfounded. There is something about the ending to the Gospel of Mark that the enemy does not want the Church to recognize. In essence, it is the mandate of the Lord Jesus for city-taking.

Verse 17a literally says that those that commit themselves to the name/purpose of the Father will be formed into a people who will accomplish His work in His way, and they will employ certain signs wherever they are planted. The Greek word utilized to depict the word **follow** is ***parakoloutheo***, which means to trace or adhere closely to the pattern of God. It is clear that the first sign that will follow those who adhere to God's plan is that devils will be "cast out." As important as personal deliverance is to the individual, this passage speaks of a much larger measure of demonic eviction. Whenever people commit themselves to the heart of God in prayer, they will be given directives concerning the Kingdom of God becoming established on this earth.

After the enemy is thrown out, the original purposes of God for the earth will be realized. Jesus' parting words in Mark's final chapter are a telling example of what will happen as praying saints remove their enemy from power and establish tabernacles of commune with God. In context, the new tongues referred to in Verse 17b refers to the process of restoring the places of commune with the Most High on His planet.

Anyone following the Lord will have a great commitment to His purpose, and their life will be continually refined in order that they might best accomplish that purpose. Jesus defined this very principle to His disciples when He taught them how to pray.

What Does It Mean To Align With God?

Matthew 6:9-13 is traditionally known as the Lord's Prayer. In this passage, Jesus outlines in a simple and undeniable fashion steps of prayer that are foundational. The church has traditionally done an injustice to this passage in that we have prayed this as a literal prayer instead of utilizing it as a model for prayer. In verse ten, Jesus speaks of how we are to align with God.

> *Thy kingdom come. Thy will be done in earth, as it is in heaven.*
> *Matthew 6:10*

God's Kingdom is to be welcomed, and in this process of the coming of the Kingdom, the enemy forces that are currently ensconced in the midst of our terrain will be dismantled and put to flight. There are very real giants in these valleys, but God will intervene on our behalf to gain victory after victory.

ENEMY: The Prince Of This World

The prince of this world is a very real and active enemy ruler. Scripture affirms his existence, and we have a responsibility to deal with this principality. Jesus spoke of the prince of this world before he encountered him in the Garden of Gethsemane:

> *Hereafter I will not talk much with you: for the prince of this world cometh, and hath nothing in me.*
>
> *John 14:30*

Some would argue that the influence of this being was destroyed at the cross; however, the Scriptures disagree with that argument. Jesus, our Lord, cites a warfare that will occur only after Pentecost. This is a post-resurrection assignment that is after the victory of Calvary.

> *Nevertheless I tell you the truth; It is expedient for you that I go away: for if I go not away, the Comforter will not come unto you; but if I depart, I will send him unto you. [8] And **when he is come**, he will reprove the world of sin, and of righteousness, and of judgment: [9] Of sin,*

> *because they believe not on me; [10] Of righteousness, because I go to my Father, and ye see me no more; [11] Of judgment, because the prince of this world is judged.*
> John 16:7-11

How Does The Prince Of This World Operate?

This demonic prince has developed strongholds throughout the world. These are closely patterned after God's original purposes for the earth when it was initially created. Each particular stronghold characterizes a particular type of debauchery or evil, and multitudes of people are enslaved.

The Holy Ghost has shined a light on the entrapments of this being who utilizes latent passions within the hearts of men and women to ensnare them. In most cases, these passions are perversions of unrealized or undeveloped anointings and giftings from the Father. The Apostle Paul spoke of this same demonic being as the god of this world who enslaves the unsaved.

> *But if our gospel be hid, it is hid to them that are lost: [4] In whom the god of this world hath blinded the minds of them which believe not, lest the light of the glorious gospel of Christ, who is the image of God, should shine unto them.*
> 2 Corinthians 4:3-4

These verses depict the depravity that we see in our cities and nations. People with extraordinary talents and abilities are entrapped by this enemy and then utilize their gifts for the sake of sin and darkness.

We must identify these strongholds as God reveals their existence. We must boldly go forth in intercessory and prophetic judgment to tear down these strongholds and to establish righteousness in their place.

The prince of this world will attempt to withstand leaders and captains of God's armies. He will strategize on unrepentant passions and will attempt to destroy the ministry of people and movements by turning the strength the Lord has placed within them into weakness.

ENEMY: The Beelzebub Force

One of the most informative dialogues concerning spiritual warfare is found in the eleventh chapter of the Gospel of St. Luke. Within this passage, Jesus instructs the disciples regarding the manner in which strongholds are taken. He also acknowledges the existence of an enemy prince known as Beelzebub.

The strongholds which are currently ruled over by the prince of this world are held together and re-supplied by this being known as Beelzebub. Jesus acknowledged his existence in three of the Gospels and never disputed his proper name or the designation of his rank and authority. This "prince" or "chief of devils" is a very real and powerful agent of the enemy.

And he was casting out a devil, and it was dumb. And it came to pass, when the devil was gone out, the dumb spake; and the people wondered. [15] But some of them said, He casteth out devils through Beelzebub the chief of the devils. [16] And others, tempting him, sought of him a sign from heaven. [17] But he, knowing their thoughts, said unto them, Every kingdom divided against itself is brought to desolation; and a house divided against a house falleth. [18] If Satan also be divided against himself, how shall his kingdom stand? because ye say that I cast out devils through Beelzebub. [19] And if I by Beelzebub cast out devils, by whom do your sons cast them out? therefore shall they be your judges. [20] But if I with the finger of God cast out devils, no doubt the kingdom of God is come upon you. [21] When a strong man armed keepeth his palace, his goods are in peace: [22] But when a stronger than he shall come upon him, and overcome him, he taketh from him all his armour wherein he trusted, and divideth his spoils. [23] He that is not with me is against me: and he that gathereth not with me scattereth. [24] When the unclean spirit is gone out of a man, he walketh through dry places, seeking rest; and finding none, he saith, I will return unto my house whence I came out. [25] And when he cometh, he findeth it swept and garnished. [26] Then goeth he, and taketh to him seven other spirits more wicked than himself; and they enter in, and dwell there: and the last state of that man is worse than the first.

Luke 11:14-26

Unity And Disunity In The Church

Just as in the realm of the church, agreement and accord is absolutely necessary for survival and creativity within the enemy camp. In Luke 11:15, the Lord introduces this idea into his discussion regarding Beelzebub. Truly, this entity oversees the order and continuity of supply within the enemy camp. He is the principality responsible for the ongoing operation of these camps or strongholds, and he maintains the proper authority structure as well. Being a strategist of structure, he guards against division in his own ranks and is an expert in creating division within the Body of Christ.

Beelzebub does not want the church to go on the offensive, which would mean a systematic dismantling of his entrusted outlay of strongholds. In this same discussion in Luke 11:23, Jesus said that there is an influence of gathering and scattering involved. Beelzebub's main goal is to stop the church from coming against his strongholds in unity; therefore, his primary strategy is scattering and sowing unrest.

How Does Beelzebub Operate?

Since the modus of prayer is communication with God, it primarily utilizes vocal abilities. These same vocal abilities are what the enemy will attempt to turn for his counterattack. He would love nothing more than to render the church *deaf* to the voice of God and *dumb* to the possibility of declaration.

This is how Beelzebub keeps the church enslaved. He wants the words of the believer to be unintelligible, without power in the spirit realm, while devastatingly disruptive in the natural.

After a local Body accepts a mandate for prayer and intercession, alarms go off in the enemy camp, and words will come forth about the church no longer caring for the people. The enemy will see to it that there are many diversionary needs and loud cries regarding such perceived needs. Most of the church will feel unable to provide assistance but will be laden with pity and mercy.

Jesus encountered this scenario when he came down from the Mount of Transfiguration and found His disciples powerless in their attempt to help a demonically possessed little boy. What could be more heart-rending than a possessed child and a desperate father? The enemy specializes in creating scenarios that are nothing more than diversions. Playing right into the hand of the enemy, people with a mercy gifting become mobilized to assist those in disarray. The words of the "forsaken ones" penetrate their caring hearts with deadly accuracy. Much like those who gathered around the little possessed boy, there is great confusion.

Within the church, similar scenarios will cause tale-bearing and gossip. Soon, strife will begin to engender itself within the Body and accusations will be hurled against the leadership. In fact, the assaults of the enemy are ultimately aimed at leadership. The objective is to apply enough "people-pleasing" pressure to keep them from moving forward within the things of God.

Churches are invariably founded on the principle of service; however, we regularly misappropriate the identity of who we are to be serving. We forget that we are to be serving God and wrongly assume that a church exists solely to serve people.

The Usurping Of The Power Of Mercy

Mercy is a commodity that the enemy does not possess in his arsenal as it flows fresh from the Throne of God.

> *Let us therefore come boldly unto the throne of grace, that we may obtain mercy, and find grace to help in time of need.*
> *Hebrews 4:16*

Mercy is an incredibly powerful commodity. It makes possible the flow of grace and enables an atmosphere wherein miracles occur. From the perspective of the enemy, the flow of mercy must be thwarted in some manner. To do this, he cannot raid the source as he already attempted to take the Throne of God but failed miserably. Since he cannot dam the mercy flow from God's Throne, his only recourse is to access and pervert the mercy giftings that are within the people of God. He does this most easily by causing the believer to confuse man's mercy with God's mercy.

Although God's mercy does not resemble man's mercy, discerning the perversion of mercy is not easy. God's mercy provides the opportunity for man to grow in grace toward the fulfillment of God's purposes. Man's mercy is generally an enablement and merely provides a temporary fix or bandage. God's mercy is rooted in the Spirit, while man's mercy is empowered by earthly viewpoints and emotional inclinations.

Jesus said when we know the truth, it will set us free. Knowing that the enemy is moving in this way and accepting this truth into our operative existence will be essential in the battle of prayer. Adhering to this understanding as a lifestyle will safeguard us from consistent frustration and failure.

Two Weapons Against Beelzebub

Within this eleventh chapter of Luke, we find two primary weapons that can be utilized against the influences of Beelzebub. These are also two major ingredients that will help the church to remain in harmony and agreement. They are the purpose of God and prophetic insight.

The purpose of God is depicted in Jesus' discussion regarding God's finger. The finger of God depicts the creative pronouncement of the purposes of our God. The finger of God is a grand study in Scripture, but this facet was ably demonstrated by the giving of the Ten Commandments by God's finger. Why would the finger of God be an expressed weapon of choice against the influence of Beelzebub? Simply, everything stems from God's purpose. Beelzebub serves to enforce an abandoning of the original purposes of God. Therefore, when we establish the purpose of our Father, Beelzebub is vanquished from the enemy holdings that he is pledged to supply and unify.

Second, we must have prophetic insight. According to Verse 17, Jesus knew the thoughts of the people. He was familiar with the overall structure of what he was dealing with, and He knew what God the Father wanted to accomplish in that scenario. Revelation 19:10 tells us that *"the testimony of Jesus is the spirit of prophecy."* In order to ascertain "What Would Jesus Do?" we must become activated in the prophetic. This is the only way to gain the present truth that will accomplish the "greater works" of Christ in the world today.

Prophecy is vital in the battle to eradicate Beelzebub because a prophetic insight relates the current **rhema** of God's purpose for the moment of need. In other words, we need to establish God's purpose, and prophecy reveals the junctures of the purpose to us and to our immediate situation.

Assaulting The Gates Of Beelzebub And The Prince Of This World

When Jesus spoke of the strongman in Luke 11:21, he was not necessarily limiting His remarks to the individual deliverance at hand, but to the larger picture of the enemy kingdom controlled by the prince of this world and enforced by Beelzebub. He lists a progression of warfare strategy that we need to recognize as part of the *paga* intercessory calling.

Beelzebub and his cohorts currently reside at rest in much of the world. They enjoy the blissful existence that only anonymity can provide. The Father wants to reveal a time frame, a plan, and an empowerment that causes the intercessor to "come upon" the enemy. This is not random or impulsive. It is a directed assault. The *paga* or divers intercessors are going to receive stirrings and giftings from the Father that will lead them to this type of pursuit.

When God called our church to be a center of intercession, He soon began to reveal Himself in ways that I had not initially expected. One day during my morning prayer time, God said He wanted to show me how He viewed Dallas. At the conclusion of that prayer time, I drove through our city. As I made my way toward the downtown skyline, I was compelled to intercede in a divers capacity at various places along the way. Some locations produced a mournful response, others triggered anger of a righteous dimension, and yet others brought prophetic insight as to controlling forces and subsequent enemy strategies.

I understood God was telling me that Dallas was His city and that He was looking for someone who was willing to partner with Him in taking it back for the Kingdom of Heaven. Over the course of the next two years, the Lord gave our warriors strategic missions within the Metroplex area. This involved many hours of research into the archives of our city library. The Holy Ghost guided us to places where the enemy had gained footholds within our city throughout the early years of Dallas' existence.

Invariably, these findings led us through steps of identificational repentance. God also gave us specific verses to declare and prophetic acts to perform unto Him all for the purpose of reclaiming the city for God. We are still in the beginning stages of this process, but we have seen some very real breakthroughs in strategic areas of our city. We continue to press onward knowing that we are in the will of God and subject to His timetable.

For most of my lifetime, I have watched the church participate in evangelistic campaigns that were well meaning but ineffective. We might gain a precious soul here or there, but the city itself was not changed at all. It is time for the Church to do things in a different manner. We must seek the Father for the keys to the city in which we live. When God's plans are followed, the enemy strongholds will be defeated. The sinful power that controlled neighborhoods can be turned to a power for righteousness. The people and giftings that once served the rulers of darkness can then be free to choose to worship the King of Kings.

The ministry of the Holy Ghost within the believer must include a ministry of evangelism. It will also include a reception of assignments of righteous import. It will not avoid the responsibility to destroy the framework of the prince of this world.

Entire areas of each city and community are famous for particular types of evil and perversion. God wants to evict these foul influences that control these locales. He wants His light to shine into this darkness. He is looking for a partner or a church full of partners who will cooperate with Him in restoring His Kingdom within the place that they are planted. This major battle plan of evangelism for the end times is a city-taking anointing. It is also a nation-taking anointing and a continent-taking anointing. Whenever the Kingdom is taken by violent intercession and strategic prophetic obedience, evangelism will be widespread. Whoever controls the watchtower controls the harvest field.

Gideon was a man that God saw hiding behind a winepress while attempting to glean morsels of wheat in secret. The Midianites were in control of God's property and God was looking for a champion on earth with which to partner. Gideon was that man. Are we Gideons hiding behind our personal winepress gleaning a little bit for the Kingdom? Or are we Gideons who encounter the vision of the Most High God and subsequently drive the enemy out of the land?

What is the interpretive significance of Gideon hiding behind a winepress while attempting to glean wheat? Simply, the picture represents the fact that most of the modern church is sustained by yesterday's wine. Because there is no fresh romance and inebriation by the wine of the Spirit, we hide our heads from the existence of a real enemy force.

While Gideon's hiding depicts the reality that he was concerned for his very life, it also indicates that he was clinging to the revelation of yesterday's glory. With an angel standing beside him, he asks about the miracles of his forefathers. We have also relegated the angels to some bygone era or to the days of the Canon of Scripture.

> *And Gideon said unto him, Oh my Lord, if the LORD be with us, why then is all this befallen us? and where be all his miracles which our fathers told us of, saying, Did not the LORD bring us up from Egypt? but now the LORD hath forsaken us, and delivered us into the hands of the Midianites.*
>
> *Judges 6:13*

God is looking for a person, an intercessor, who will stand in the gap and make up the hedge today. The area where the enemy used to break through will now be the place where we make a stand for God. Greater is He who is in us than he that is in the world.

Divers Tongues

chapter 13

A Different Kind Of Worship

Exact Songs – Oide Pneumatikos

Spiritual songs are a lost commodity to much of the Church. We have become packaged and intellectual in our worship and perceive anything other than a stylized approach as being unprepared.

God wants us to sing to Him in spiritual songs. This involves pure devotion to Him. We must abandon the rigidity of scheduled services, yielding only to the Holy Spirit and not to public scrutiny.

When we began to thirst for this process in our church, it was met with both love and hatred. Some people said that it was the most exhilarating mode of worship that they had ever known. Others decried the process as robbing them of the ability to worship God the way they always had. Disinterest begat boredom, which begat non-participation, which begat criticism, which begat hatred of anything that upset their traditional framework of worship. Truly the mind will display its enmity towards the things of the Spirit.

I remember the first time that I uttered a message in tongues in a public meeting. It was a frighteningly liberating experience for me. To allow my spirit to commune with and on behalf of God in a public setting was remarkable. Over time, I had become so familiar with my utterances that I lost the adventurousness of my passion before God.

I also remember the time that I first sang a spiritual song in my church. We had just finished a standard and well-known chorus, but I felt that there was an unusual stirring of the Holy Ghost. Instructing our pianist to chord for a while, I waited on the Lord. When I began to sing what was on my heart, there was an exhilaration that flooded me. I think that I nearly scared our musicians to death as they had no lead sheets to follow. It was at that moment that I knew the difference between being a song leader and being a worship leader.

There seems to be little consideration given for the flow of the Holy Spirit in traditional worship and even less creativity of expression. Often, no allowance is made for the time involved in waiting on the Lord. Most people have little tolerance for what is revealed to "others that sit by."

Spiritual songs need to be welcomed and they need to be pioneered into a dormant church. I grew up singing the old hymns and I love them. I can still quote all of those songs today. Yet, there is something candidly wrong with a church that is *only* inspired by songs that focus on events or themes of emphasis from the last two centuries. When we do not allow God the time and opportunity to express His heart in new and spontaneous song, we lose our passion to a large degree. In this oversight, the church is robbed of vitality through ignorance, disobedience or fear.

Oide pneumatikos are spiritual songs. They are also "odes" to God and are referenced mainly in Ephesians 5:19: *"Speaking to yourselves in psalms and hymns and* **spiritual**

songs [oide pneumatikos], *singing and making melody in your heart to the Lord,"* and Colossians 3:16: *"Let the word of Christ dwell in you richly in all wisdom; teaching and admonishing one another in psalms and hymns and* **spiritual songs** [oide pneumatikos], *singing with grace in your hearts to the Lord."*

When we speak of an ode, it is generally a very lively or very sorrowful poem set to music about an exploit of a great man, woman or people group. Commemorations of impassioned theme songs mark the histories of many famous wars. In the Civil War, the North sang "John Brown's Body" set to the tune of "The Battle Hymn of the Republic" and was opposed by Southern bands who played the lively "Dixie." World War I had "Over There" and World War II enjoyed countless melodies with compelling verses of poetic import. Individuals such as Daniel Boone and Davy Crockett are immortalized with odes to their exploits.

Why should we not gain inspiration from our God who does new and magnificent acts each day? God speaks eloquently and beautifully in every service where He is worshipped and adored. He wants us to be able to love Him, hear Him and sing or declare what He is expressing to us.

> *To the chief Musician upon Shoshannim, for the sons of Korah, Maschil, A Song of loves. My heart is inditing a good matter: I speak of the things which I have made touching the king: my tongue is the pen of a ready writer.*
>
> *Psalm 45:1*

This is the essence of *oide pneumatikos*. Our tongue must convey what His heart communicates to ours. Out of the abundance of our heart, our lips must speak and sing. Whether it is song, prophetic expression, or interpretive dance, we must be ready and willing to let the Holy Ghost create our praise during every one of our services of worship to the Lord.

Warfare And Strategy

Spiritual songs can express current battle fervor and strategy as well as serve as a mighty weapon before our enemies. Do you think that the Levites who were placed at the head of the army of the king faced the enemy with hymnals in their hands? Do you think they were singing about something that happened decades before? Or do you believe that they might have been firmly focused on what God was saying *right then*?

A case of this sort is found in the New Testament when Paul and Silas were imprisoned at the midnight hour.

> *And at midnight Paul and Silas prayed, and sang praises unto God: and the prisoners heard them. [26] And suddenly there was a great earthquake, so that the foundations of the prison were shaken: and immediately all the doors were opened, and every one's bands were loosed.*
>
> *Acts 16:25-26*

Do you think that they sang the latest from Nashville? Or do you believe that the earthquake-inducing melody came in a present truth reality through their heart?

The world has captured this demonstration of battle fervor. The Confederate soldier had the "rebel yell," which cannot be recalled but could only be evoked from the passionate response to pending battle. The American Indians sang war songs and danced war dances. Their blood-curdling melodies and legendary yelps struck fear into the hearts of their enemies. The ancient Irish, with their boron drums and various instruments, sang powerful tunes to frighten the enemy and inspire themselves for warfare. It is time for the Church to rise up in this same warlike fervor and draw upon the innate passion deep within their spirits to declare the purpose of the Lord.

A Return To Vulnerability Before God

Spiritual songs imply vulnerability to God and a willingness to be humble before an audience of people. To allow God to sing through us about Him in an "unpracticed" mode is a foreign and uncomfortable concept to most music or worship leaders. Our training stresses the necessity of preparedness and discourages the desire to be spontaneous before God.

King David declared that he would not offer unto God sacrifices that cost him nothing. He also said that the place of sacrifice would be bought with a price.

And the king said unto Araunah, Nay; but I will surely buy it of thee at a price: neither will I offer burnt offerings unto the Lord my God of that which doth cost me nothing. So David bought the threshingfloor and the oxen for fifty shekels of silver.

2 Samuel 24:24

The Word says that we need to strive for masteries as well as study and prepare ourselves in order that our workmanship not be characterized as shoddy or embarrassing to our employer or customer. There is a real place for preparation, study and practice. This represents the price of the threshing floor.

The sacrifice should cost *you* something. When David led the Ark of God into the Holy City, it cost him something. The Levites had faithfully offered sacrifice every six steps along the journey. This represented an adherence to established revelation. David's dance was an expression of devotion to God from his heart. David proclaimed afterward that he was not only prepared to do the same demonstration again but to be even more base (2 Samuel 6:13, 14, 22). True worship involves both the mind and the spirit.

When we come before God, we should be prepared. Our gifts and talents should be honed in adoration to Him, and we should be absolutely vulnerable to allow the Spirit of God to flow in mighty fashion through **oide pneumatikos**.

The Tabernacle Of David

Amos 9:11 says that the Tabernacle of David will be rebuilt. The Tabernacle of Moses represented the law, but the Tabernacle of David represents true heartfelt praise and worship. It represents the commune with the Heavenly Father for which David was famous.

For the Church to welcome the rebuilding of the Tabernacle of David, we must be willing to become spiritual in our worship. David appointed three men to officiate in the Tabernacle, Asaph, Heman and Jeduthun. These men were very talented and skilled in musical expression. What set them apart for leadership under David's supervision was that they were all classified as "seers" (1 Chronicles 25:5; 2 Chronicles 29:30; 35:15).

Seers can grasp the spirit realm as the Lord opens their eyes to conceptualize what is outside of the eye of this natural world. They possess a unique perspective that is often misconstrued or characterized as being bizarre. For that reason, seers normally are told to "get real" by those who are not similarly gifted. Since the gift is not generally welcomed and developed, it can promote rebellion or an abnormal or stunted personality. Consequently, they are often recruited by the enemy, and sometimes they just become social outcasts. What a tragedy, especially since much of this maligning occurs at the hands of the Church.

David and his chief musicians were seers. If they were around today, they would probably not be afforded many "gigs" within the Church. Seeing into the spirit realm should be a normal occurrence at worship gatherings. Imagine the concept of requiring a "seer" gifting for ministry in music! It was essential for David in offering the kind of worship that touched the heart of God, and it is essential for establishing Davidic worship today.

Divers Tongues

chapter 14

A More Excellent Way

Not Just A Poem

Perhaps the most powerful chapter in the Book of 1 Corinthians is the thirteenth, and perhaps none is more misunderstood and misapplied. Some critics will declare that this chapter on love removes the necessity of speaking in tongues because Paul introduces the writing as "a more excellent way." Thankfully for those who believe in the ongoing validity of the gifts of the Spirit, the thirteenth chapter is sandwiched between two chapters that detail the usage of spiritual gifts within the Church.

This wonderful chapter is often relegated to the docile climate of weddings or the sober reality of a funeral. While prophetically poetic, this mighty passage speaks most powerfully of the abiding and compelling power of God's love. The word for **charity** is translated from the Greek word *agape*. *Agape,* or the love that our Father provides, is the most important element in our lives.

When these thirteen verses are fully actualized, the message of this simple book becomes meaningful and effective. Herein we find the framework through which the gifts of the Spirit operate. When the believer properly accesses *agape*, we find our place in God. The meaning of our existence is then revealed, and an empowerment to accomplish that meaning is released. Just as the fruits of the Spirit reveal our character, the gifts of the Spirit reveal our purpose.

Progressions Of Importance

Observe the progression of the first two verses:

> *Though I speak with the tongues of men and of angels, and have not charity, I am become as sounding brass, or a tinkling cymbal. [2] And though I have the gift of prophecy, and understand all mysteries, and all knowledge; and though I have all faith, so that I could remove mountains, and have not charity, I am nothing.*
> 1 Corinthians 13:1-2

The tongues of men and angels can be none other than a depiction of the divers tongues capacity. What empowers divers tongues is the relationship with God's love. If we have any other motive than relationship, divers tongues will have no real meaning. Without a love relationship with the Father, divers tongues is nothing more than dynamic "sounding brass" or intimate "tinkling cymbals." **Agape** empowers divers tongues and grants a purpose for the exchange of communication.

As we communicate in love with the Father, we begin to know His meaning for our lives and for the place wherein we live. Interpreting our relationship with God and making this information known is the meaning of prophecy in this passage. Even the power of this revelation is insignificant if devoid of the relational love of the Father.

Prophecy will involve the uncovering of mysteries and the communication of the knowledge acquired from those discoveries. This understanding will inspire belief and motivate individuals to take great steps of obedient faith. Through this process, mountains of enemy opposition and obstacles will be removed. Even though this process is exciting and purpose laden, without *agape* as our driving force and motivation, we are nothing. Love begins the process, is the impetus throughout, and is what brings meaning and fulfillment. No matter what we learn or accomplish, if we lose the *agape* that provided the iniation and fruition, we have failed.

The New Testament church at Ephesus was the pre-eminent example of love gained and lost. The Epistle of Paul to the Ephesians provides us with essential knowledge pertaining to the spirit realm, our place within the heavenlies, spiritual weaponry and warfare, and a host of other fantastic insights. The Ephesians patterned the progression of mysteries revealed and prophetic understanding and application. This knowledge was revealed by virtue of their heart of love before the Heavenly Father. However, in the Book of Revelation, Jesus rebuked them for losing their way.

> *Nevertheless I have somewhat against thee, because thou hast left thy first love.*
> *Revelation 2:4*

Without a sustained pursuit of passion, they degenerated into nothingness.

> *Charity never faileth: but whether there be prophecies, they shall fail; whether there be tongues, they shall cease; whether there be knowledge, it shall vanish away.*
> *1 Corinthians 13:8*

The revelations of God are mighty and fulfilling, but they are only useful for the hour in which they are revealed. Only the passion for the One who gives the revelation will remain. Even those who are inclined to dramatic modes of philanthropic or sacrificial service in the name of the Father can lose Him if they do not regularly focus on His love. In the same way, benevolent and social demonstrations will lose their meaning if the relationship with God is lost, and demonstrations of goodwill done *for* God instead of *with* Him will lose the heart of ***agape***.

> *And though I bestow all my goods to feed the poor, and though I give my body to be burned, and have not charity, it profiteth me nothing.*
> *1 Corinthians 13:3*

Progression Into Maturity

Consider with me the maturation process that is outlined in Verse 11:

> *When I was a child, I spake as a child, I understood as a child, I thought as a child: but when I became a man, I put away childish things.*
> *1 Corinthians 13:11*

How graphic a depiction of the way God moves in and through us. We begin as uninformed children, but our understanding and thoughts begin to be identified and developed. As each new progression of truth materializes within us, we are matured. As this maturation process continues, we will put away the things of yesterday that are no longer current in the ongoing move of the Lord in our lives.

All That Matters

The love of the Father is the only thing that matters. Nothing else has meaning, and nothing else will abide. The entire reason to adapt divers tongues is to know the Father more intimately and to serve the Father in a more effective fashion. This is a gift and office like no other.

As this chapter concludes reflectively, so will your life and ministry. You were born again in order that you might become alive to a relationship with the Heavenly Father. Divers tongues will open you into new realms of commune and devotion to the Father of Love. Let this be your conclusion and beginning.

PNEUMATIKOS PUBLISHING
P.O. Box 595351
Dallas, Texas 75359
(214) 821-5290

To order additional copies of this book or other books published by Pneumatikos Publishing:
◊ call us at (214) 821-5290
◊ email at info@pneumatikos.com
◊ order online at www.pneumatikos.com

BOOKS YOU NEED TO READ!!

Divers Tongues
By Ronald W. Crawford

The author, a seasoned pastor, takes us through God's Word as he explores the possibilities that are both wondrous and compelling. We must have the gift of divers tongues.

Ministering with Angels
By Paul David Harrison

One of the distinguishing characteristics of the culminating events in God's timetable will be the influx of the angelic in our churches and individual lives. They are coming at God's bidding to impart gifts and anointings reserved for these last days.

~~S.W. 48~~
Spiritual Warfare 48
Communion 2
Intimacy 2
Complacency 52
Holiness 66, 67
Communication 74
Body Language 74
Praise, show forth 74
Authority 1, 86, 87, 98
Unity 87
Leadership 87
Structure 87
Faith 93
Unbelief 93